Guitar Strumming Patterns

Easy-to-Use • Easy-to-Carry
Internet Audio Links

Jake Jackson & Phil Dawson

FLAME TREE
PUBLISHING

Publisher and Creative Director: Nick Wells
Project Editor: Gillian Whitaker
Layout Design: Jane Ashley
New Musical Examples: Phil Dawson

20 22 24 23 21
1 3 5 7 9 10 8 6 4 2

This edition first published 2020 by
FLAME TREE PUBLISHING
6 Melbray Mews
London SW6 3NS
United Kingdom
www.flametreepublishing.com
Music website: www.flametreemusic.com

© 2020 Flame Tree Publishing Ltd

ISBN 978-1-83964-190-9

A CIP record for this book is available from the British Library upon request.

Acknowledgements
All images and diagrams © Flame Tree Publishing, except the following: Shutterstock.com and courtesy
Simon Kadula 6, 379; VALUA STUDIO 11; Marina Andrejchenko 13; Beatriz Vera 33; the goatman 47;
maradon 333 63; PR Image Factory 91; Peter's eyes 93; SeventyFour 97, 111; Lukas Gojda 113; Roma
Voloshyn 133; Dmytro Zinkevych 155; simona pilolla 2 175; Mr Wright Photography 195; Alexander
Raths 211; Antonio Guillem 224; MBLifestyle 229; optimarc 243; Olaf Speier 245; stoszko 247; ieang
251; Dmytro Buianskyi 273; ntkris 325; LightField Studios 329; SMEEitz 338; silverkblackstock 358.
Android, iPhone, iPad, Nokia, Samsung and Galaxy S are all trademarks or registered trademarks.

Jake Jackson is a musician and writer of practical music books. He has created and
contributed to over 30 practical music books, including *How to Play Guitar* and the
bestselling *Guitar Chord* and *Piano Chord* titles.

Phil Dawson is a guitarist, composer and teacher whose work encompasses a variety of
touring, recording, film and TV work as an instrumentalist, bandleader, music writer and
producer. He's also a lecturer and mentor at a variety of educational levels, and devisor of
several courses for instrumentalists, bands and studio musicians. See his work at
www.phildawsonmusic.co.uk.

Printed in China

Contents

Introduction

As well as providing a variety of strumming and picking patterns across musical genres, this book includes examples of them in use, and offers advice on general technique, rhythm, and chord knowledge. The patterns and examples are divided by genre and range from one bar to 12 bars in length, to give maximum flexibility.

Chapter 1 (Basics) gives an overview of the musical styles, rhythm notation, and types of diagrams covered in this book.

Chapter 2 (Folk & Country) dives right in with six different Folk & Country strum patterns, and four different picking patterns to try. Also includes examples of them in use.

Chapter 3 (Blues, Soul & R&B) includes a great selection of Blues, Soul and Funk strum patterns, with notational examples of them applied to simple chords.

Chapter 4 (Rock'n'Roll) covers three distinct strumming patterns for this popular music style, with a few examples of them in action in twelve-bar sequences. Also introduces a common chord progression for you to try for this style.

Chapter 5 (Pop Rock) contains a bunch of useful patterns for this genre, inspired by some pop greats. Includes examples of them in use with common chord progressions.

Chapter 6 (Metal, Prog & Heavy Rock) gives a range of riffs from Rock's roots in Blues Rock, all the way to Prog Rock and Heavy Metal strum patterns. Includes examples and variations to try at your leisure.

Chapter 7 (Alternative Rock) offers several strum and picking patterns for the alternative rock genre, encompassing Indie Rock, Punk, and Grunge, with examples for each.

Chapter 8 (Other Styles) covers strum patterns for additional musical styles, such as Samba, Reggae and Swing.

Chapter 9 (Skills) looks at some useful techniques for the non-fretting hand: learn how to master slides, plectrum use, string damping, smooth chord changes and more.

Chapter 10 (Rhythm) provides guidance on basic timing, note and rest values, time signatures, rhythm notation and pulse.

Chapter 11 (Chords) acts as reference for common chord types, symbols, keys, and chord progressions. This chapter also looks at how to apply this knowledge of basic and more advanced chords to the strumming examples in this book.

Chapter 12 (More Resources) lists a glossary of terms, companion books, and our website flametreemusic.com.

Basics

Folk

Blues

Rock 'n'Roll

Pop Rock

Heavy Rock

Alt. Rock

Other Styles

Skills

Rhythm

Chords

More

1

Basics

Before getting your teeth into the strumming
and picking patterns, this chapter introduces
some of the diagrams you'll come across in this
book. It also gives a reminder of standard and
TAB notation, guitar notes, rhythm notation,
and common symbols to watch out for in the
patterns and examples.

Basics

Folk

Blues

Rock
'n'Roll

Pop
Rock

Heavy
Rock

Alt.
Rock

Other
Styles

Skills

Rhythm

Chords

More

Basics

Folk

Blues

Rock
'n'Roll

Pop
Rock

Heavy
Rock

Alt.
Rock

Other
Styles

Skills

Rhythm

Chords

More

Musical Styles

The strum and picking patterns in this book cover the following musical genres:

Folk & Country – including bluegrass rhythm and basic picking styles like Travis and Clawhammer.

Blues, Soul & R&B – including the Twelve-bar Blues and Funk.

Rock'n'Roll – some popular simple rhythms and examples in this style.

Pop Rock – inspired by the likes of David Bowie, Dire Straits, and The Beatles.

Metal, Prog & Heavy Rock – from Blues Rock to Heavy Metal.

Basics

Folk

Blues

Rock
'n'Roll

Pop
Rock

Heavy
Rock

Alt.
Rock

Other
Styles

Skills

Rhythm

Chords

More

Alternative –including Indie Rock, Punk and Grunge styles.

Other Styles – including Samba, Reggae and Swing.

Basics

Folk

Blues

Rock
'n'Roll

Pop
Rock

Heavy
Rock

Alt.
Rock

Other
Styles

Skills

Rhythm

Chords

More

Getting Started
The Fretboard

When dealing with chords it's useful to have a clear idea of where each note lies in relation to other notes. On the guitar, the frets are organized in semitone intervals:

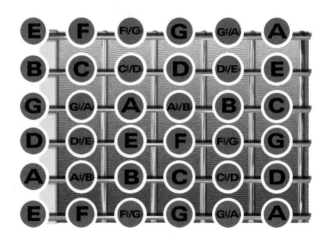

Guitar fingerboard with nut on the left, bass strings at the bottom, high E string at the top

Guitar Chord Diagrams

The bass E appears on the left (6th string)

The top E is on the right (1st string)

Basics

Folk

Blues

Rock
'n'Roll

Pop
Rock

Heavy
Rock

Alt.
Rock

Other
Styles

Skills

Rhythm

Chords

More

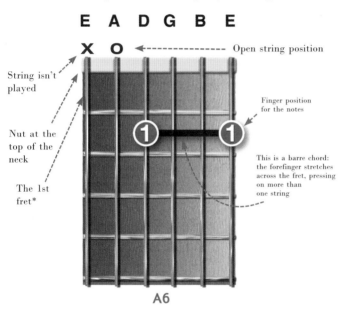

E A D G B E

X O ←------------ Open string position

String isn't played

Nut at the top of the neck

The 1st fret*

Finger position for the notes

This is a barre chord: the forefinger stretches across the fret, pressing on more than one string

A6

1 is the index finger   **2** is the middle finger

3 is the ring finger   **4** is the little finger

* When the chord position isn't as close to the nut, a number to the left indicates the changed location on the fretboard. E.g. a '2' means the diagram starts from the 2nd fret rather than the 1st.

Basics

Folk

Blues

Rock 'n'Roll

Pop Rock

Heavy Rock

Alt. Rock

Other Styles

Skills

Rhythm

Chords

More

Standard Notation

In this book there are several instances where chords are shown in practice, as part of a piece of short music. While some musical knowledge is assumed, the below is provided as a quick reminder of how music is recorded in standard musical notation.

The Treble Clef

The pitch of a note is indicated by where it is positioned on the musical stave. The clef tells you which range of pitches the notes on the stave represent. The guitar and the right hand on the piano both generally use the treble clef.

Basics

Folk

Blues

Rock
'n'Roll

Pop
Rock

Heavy
Rock

Alt.
Rock

Other
Styles

Skills

Rhythm

Chords

More

The treble clef is used for instruments that sound higher, usually above middle C. It is also known the 'G' clef, as the note 'G' is signified by the line that the curl wraps around.

The curl of the treble clef wraps around the second line up from the bottom line.

5

4

3

2

1

Numbered from the bottom line upwards

Basics

Folk

Blues

Rock
'n'Roll

Pop
Rock

Heavy
Rock

Alt.
Rock

Other
Styles

Skills

Rhythm

Chords

More

TAB Notation

Some guitarists prefer to use tablature (called TAB) instead of staves.

The six lines represent the six strings of the guitar, from the high E string to the low E string, and the numbers represent the frets that produce the notes. A zero indicates that the string is played open.

In the below example, the first C is played on the 5th string – the A string – by holding down the third fret along. The D is produced by playing the 4th string open, the E is sounded by holding down the second fret on the same string, then the third fret on the same string produces the F, and so on.

Basics

Folk

Blues

Rock
'n'Roll

Pop
Rock

Heavy
Rock

Alt.
Rock

Other
Styles

Skills

Rhythm

Chords

More

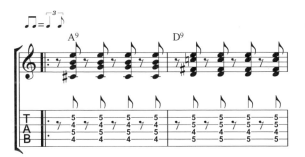

The examples in this book show chord progressions using both standard (treble clef) and TAB notation. In the above example, you can see how the length of the notes is shown in both treble and TAB staves. Not all the notes in the examples will be the same length; see more on page 30-31.

The next two pages provide a brief overview of how standard and TAB notation translate to one another, to indicate both pitch and rhythm.

Basics

Folk

Blues

Rock
'n'Roll

Pop
Rock

Heavy
Rock

Alt.
Rock

Other
Styles

Skills

Rhythm

Chords

More

Standard and TAB Notation

The main strings in standard and TAB notation are as follows:

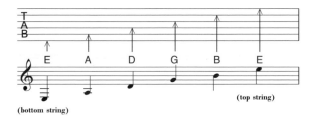

A few examples of individual notes:

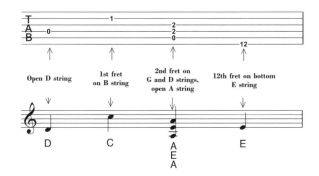

Basics

Folk

Blues

Rock
'n'Roll

Pop
Rock

Heavy
Rock

Alt.
Rock

Other
Styles

Skills

Rhythm

Chords

More

Usually the rhythm of the music is written above the stave in notes which lack noteheads:

This would be played as follows:

Whatever type of tablature is being used, if the strings are to be tuned differently, the required tuning is given at the start of the staff. For example, an alternative tuning below has the bottom string tuned to D instead of E:

Basics

Folk

Blues

Rock
'n'Roll

Pop
Rock

Heavy
Rock

Alt.
Rock

Other
Styles

Skills

Rhythm

Chords

More

Basics of Notation

Traditional music notation is written on a staff of five lines. Each line, and each space between the lines, represents a different note. Pitches higher or lower than the notes on the stave are shown using ledger lines. This diagram shows the notes from the open low E string to the E at the 12th fret on the first string.

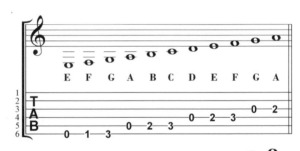

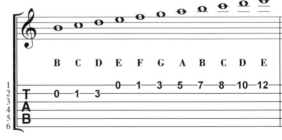

Treble Clef Line and Space Notes on the Guitar

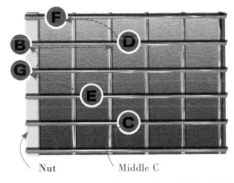

Nut   Middle C

The diagram here is from the player's view. Treble clef line notes on a guitar are spread across the strings. The notes G and B are shown here on the open strings.

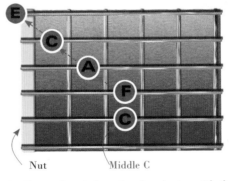

Nut   Middle C

Again, the diagram here is from the player's view with the treble clef open notes played across the strings. The top note E is shown here on the open string.

Folk

Blues

Rock 'n'Roll

Pop Rock

Heavy Rock

Alt. Rock

Other Styles

Skills

Rhythm

Chords

More

Basics

Folk

Blues

Rock
'n'Roll

Pop
Rock

Heavy
Rock

Alt.
Rock

Other
Styles

Skills

Rhythm

Chords

More

Sharps

This is the sharp sign.

It is written to the left of a notehead.

A sharpened note is half a tone higher than the note that is being sharpened.

When a sharp is written in front of a particular note all subsequent uses of that note in the bar will also be sharpened. From the beginning of the next bar, the note reverts to its previous state.

Flats

This is the flat sign.

It is written to the left of a notehead.

A flattened note is half a tone lower than the note that is being flattened.

When a flat is written in front of a particular note all subsequent uses of that note in the bar will also be flattened. From the beginning of the next bar, the note reverts to its previous state.

Basics

Folk

Blues

Rock
'n'Roll

Pop
Rock

Heavy
Rock

Alt.
Rock

Other
Styles

Skills

Rhythm

Chords

More

Basics

Folk

Blues

Rock
'n'Roll

Pop
Rock

Heavy
Rock

Alt.
Rock

Other
Styles

Skills

Rhythm

Chords

More

Naturals

This is the natural sign.

It is written to the left of a notehead.

A natural sign is used to cancel the effect of a sharp or a flat note played previously in the same bar, or present in the key signature (see page 336).

Once applied, the natural symbol for the particular note applies for the rest of the bar unless another sharp or flat appears.

Basics

Folk

Blues

Rock
'n'Roll

Pop
Rock

Heavy
Rock

Alt.
Rock

Other
Styles

Skills

Rhythm

Chords

More

Natural Notes on the Guitar

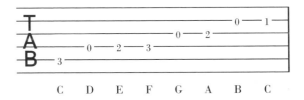

C   D   E   F   G   A   B   C

The low E string is at the bottom and the notes
are given the fret number on the appropriate string.
The natural notes are shown in TAB above and a
guitar diagram below.

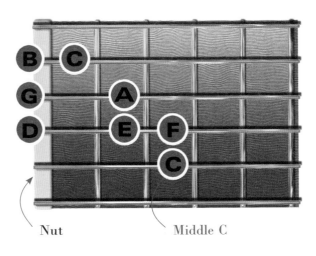

Nut   Middle C

Basics

Folk

Blues

Rock
'n'Roll

Pop
Rock

Heavy
Rock

Alt.
Rock

Other
Styles

Skills

Rhythm

Chords

More

Parts of a Note

Notes are made up of:

1. A **notehead** that is either hollow or filled.

2. A **stem**, if the note is shorter in length.

3. A **tail**, if the note is even shorter in length. The shorter the length, the more tails it has. When connecting notes of the same value, this becomes a **beam**. A semiquaver as two tails, so connects to other semiquavers using two beams.

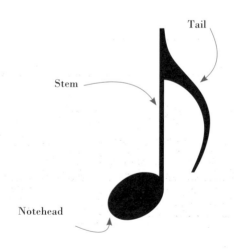

Rhythm Guitar

Knowing a number of chord shapes is useful, but it's only when you can put some of these chords together with an interesting strumming pattern, and change fluently between them, that you'll really begin to develop your rhythm-guitar technique.

Some useful skills to develop for rhythm-guitar playing, and chord playing generally include:

- The ability to keep in time, and listen closely to other instruments involved.

- Smooth chord transitions: look for links or common notes between chords.

- A clean, reliable strumming technique. Avoid gaps and build up to more inventive patterns.

- Knowledge of chord charts and rhythm charts.

Folk

Blues

Rock 'n'Roll

Pop Rock

Heavy Rock

Alt. Rock

Other Styles

Skills

Rhythm

Chords

More

Basics

Folk

Blues

Rock
'n'Roll

Pop
Rock

Heavy
Rock

Alt.
Rock

Other
Styles

Skills

Rhythm

Chords

More

Rhythm Notation

Chords can be communicated a number of different ways in music. As well as simple chord charts, they can be shown in rhythm charts, and full musical notation, both of which specify particular note durations.

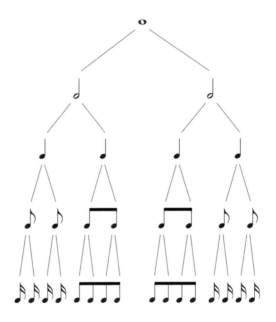

Basics

Basics

Folk

Blues

Rock
'n'Roll

Pop
Rock

Heavy
Rock

Alt.
Rock

Other
Styles

Skills

Rhythm

Chords

More

These note values also have an equivalent rest.
Below is a quick reminder of the note names and
rest symbols, with their relative lengths.

These are looked at in more detail in the Rhythm
chapter (see Note Values, Rests and Rhythm
Notation on pages 252–289). The section also covers
ties, triplets, and timing generally.

NAME	NOTE	REST	DURATION IN 4/4 TIME
Semibreve (whole note)	o	▬	4 beats
Dotted Minim	♩.	▬·	3 beats
Minim (half note)	♩	▬	2 beats
Dotted Crotchet	♩.	♩.	1½ beats
Crotchet (quarter note)	♩	♩	1 beat
Dotted Quaver	♪.	♩.	¾ beat
Quaver (eighth note)	♪	♩	½ beat
Semiquaver (sixteenth note)	♬	♩	¼ beat

Basics

Folk

Blues

Rock
'n'Roll

Pop
Rock

Heavy
Rock

Alt.
Rock

Other
Styles

Skills

Rhythm

Chords

More

Useful Symbols

Upstrum:	V
Upstrum on TAB:	↑
Downstrum:	⊓
Downstrum on TAB:	↓
Time Signatures (examples):	4/4, 3/4, 6/8
Repeat signs:	‖: :‖
Accent:	>
Slide (ascending):	╱
Slide (descending):	╲
Mute:	X
Palm Mute:	P.M.
Hammer-On:	H.O.
Staccato:	♪.

Basics

Folk

Blues

Rock 'n'Roll

Pop Rock

Heavy Rock

Alt. Rock

Other Styles

Skills

Rhythm

Chords

More

Basics

Folk

Blues

Rock
'n'Roll

Pop
Rock

Heavy
Rock

Alt.
Rock

Other
Styles

Skills

Rhythm

Chords

More

Diagrams in This Book

All the examples in this book are one of three types:

*   Strumming Patterns
*   Fingerpicking Patterns
*   Notated Examples

Strumming patterns will look like the one opposite: downstrums and upstrums are shown on a basic TAB diagram.

Fingerpicking patterns will include specific notes marked out on TAB (see page 36).

Notated examples will either show the pattern in TAB only, or they will be shown in full as both standard and TAB notation. For both types, specific chord notes and rhythm will be supplied (see page 36).

Strumming Patterns

An example of the type of strumming pattern you
will come across in this book:

tuning, string
labels

time signature

downstrum

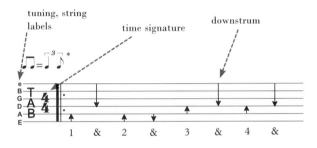

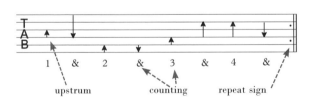

upstrum

counting

repeat sign

*indicates swung rhythm: two quavers played unequally so
that the first quaver lasts twice as long as the second, but they
are still played within the space of 2 quavers (one crotchet)

Folk

Blues

Rock
'n'Roll

Pop
Rock

Heavy
Rock

Alt.
Rock

Other
Styles

Skills

Rhythm

Chords

More

Basics

Folk

Blues

Rock 'n'Roll

Pop Rock

Heavy Rock

Alt. Rock

Other Styles

Skills

Rhythm

Chords

More

Fingerpicking Patterns

An example of the type of fingerpicking pattern you will come across in this book:

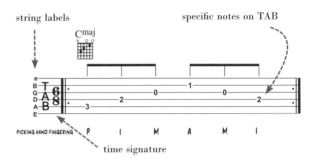

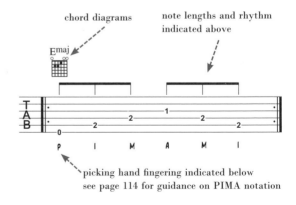

picking hand fingering indicated below
see page 114 for guidance on PIMA notation

Notated Examples

An example of the types of notated examples you will come across in this book. First, in TAB only:

Basics

Folk

Blues

Rock
'n'Roll

Pop
Rock

Heavy
Rock

Alt.
Rock

Other
Styles

Skills

Rhythm

Chords

More

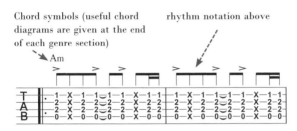

Or an example can be shown in both standard and TAB notation:

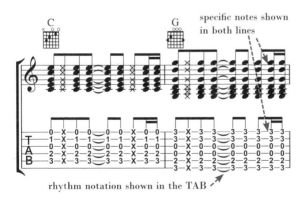

rhythm notation shown in the TAB

Basics

Folk

Blues

Rock
'n'Roll

Pop
Rock

Heavy
Rock

Alt.
Rock

Other
Styles

Skills

Rhythm

Chords

More

Sound Links

You'll need an internet-ready smartphone with a camera (e.g. iPhone, any Android phone (e.g. Samsung Galaxy, Nokia Lumia). The best results are achieved using a **WIFI** connection.

1. With the most recent phone software updates you can **use the camera to scan**. If this doesn't work you can download **any free QR code reader** from your phone's app store.

2. On your smartphone, open the app and scan the QR code whenever it appears in this book.

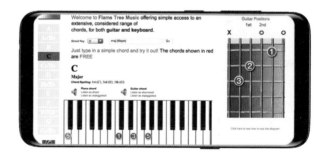

Basics

Folk

Blues

Rock
'n'Roll

Pop
Rock

Heavy
Rock

Alt.
Rock

Other
Styles

Skills

Rhythm

Chords

More

3. This will take you directly to the relevant chord on **flametreemusic.com**, where you can access and **hear** a huge library of sounds.

4. Use the drop-down menu to choose from 20 scales or **12 free chords** (50 with subscription) **per key**.

5. Click the sounds! Both piano and guitar audio is provided for whole chords and individual notes. This is particularly helpful when you're playing with others.

The QR codes give you direct access to chords and scales. You can access a much wider range of chords if you register and subscribe.

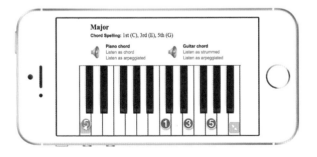

Basics

Folk

Blues

Rock
'n'Roll

Pop
Rock

Heavy
Rock

Alt.
Rock

Other
Styles

Skills

Rhythm

Chords

More

2

Folk & Country

Folk music can be described as 'the natural expression of a people'. It is rarely written for profit and is passed down from generation to generation, musician to musician. The examples in this chapter include a range of Folk & Country strumming and picking patterns, including bluegrass rhythm, basic arpeggiated picking, and basic Travis picking.

Basics

Folk

Blues

Rock 'n'Roll

Pop Rock

Heavy Rock

Alt. Rock

Other Styles

Skills

Rhythm

Chords

More

Basics

Folk

Blues

Rock 'n'Roll

Pop Rock

Heavy Rock

Alt. Rock

Other Styles

Skills

Rhythm

Chords

More

Folk and Country Music

Folk music exists in every country, whether it comes in the form of African tribal chants, Irish reels or Native American ceremonial songs. Country music grew out of American folk music and now encompasses a variety of styles, including bluegrass, traditional C&W (country and western), western swing, country rock and Americana. Most country songs are built around simple chord progressions and melodies.

Playing Folk

In folk music, acoustic guitar can be either finger-picked or strummed with a plectrum. Typical finger-pickers will normally play the bass strings with the thumb and the treble strings with the index, middle and third fingers of their picking hand. Some players just use their index and middle fingers for the treble strings, and rest their

Basics

Folk

Blues

Rock
'n'Roll

Pop
Rock

Heavy
Rock

Alt.
Rock

Other
Styles

Skills

Rhythm

Chords

More

other two fingers on the guitar body for support. Guitarists often use the same fingerpicking pattern for the whole song, although some virtuoso players adopt a more elaborate style.

Playing Country Music

Country-music acoustic guitarists employ the same techniques as folk players. However, country electric-guitar players use a lot of note bends in their solos. Of particular importance is the 'harmony bend', a pedal-steel type effect where some notes are held while another is bent. Country players also use double-stops (two-note chords), hammer-ons, pull-offs and slides to add further colour to their solos. Another specialist country technique is 'chicken picking', a damped, staccato right-hand style employed by James Burton and others for fast, funky phrases. A neat country trick is to use the guitar's volume control (or a volume pedal) to fade chords and notes in.

Basics

Folk

Blues

Rock
'n'Roll

Pop
Rock

Heavy
Rock

Alt.
Rock

Other
Styles

Skills

Rhythm

Chords

More

Guidance

Many folk flat-pickers use a plectrum to play chord arpeggios across the strings, along with scales and licks. When accompanying vocals, these players tend to strum the same rhythm for an entire song.

Flat-picking Technique

Flat-picking is a playing style in which all notes, scalic and chordal, are articulated with a plectrum or thumb pick. To strum with a plectrum, finger your chord with your fretting hand and angle the plectrum, pointing slightly upwards, in towards the strings with your picking hand. Then stroke the plectrum across the strings, making sure that all the notes in the chord ring out cleanly. Some acoustic flat-pickers can play extremely fast solos with a plectrum by alternating between upstrokes and downstrokes of the picking hand, while the fretting hand is fingering the notes.

Useful Symbols

Upstrum: V

Upstrum on TAB: ↑

Downstrum: ⊓

Downstrum on TAB: ↓

Time Signatures (examples):   **4/4, 3/4, 6/8**

Repeat signs: ‖: :‖

Accent: >

Slide (ascending):   ╱

Slide (descending):   ╲

Mute: X

Palm Mute: P.M.

Hammer-On: H.O.

Staccato: ♩.

Basics

Folk

Blues

Rock 'n'Roll

Pop Rock

Heavy Rock

Alt. Rock

Other Styles

Skills

Rhythm

Chords

More

Basics

Folk

Blues

Rock 'n'Roll

Pop Rock

Heavy Rock

Alt. Rock

Other Styles

Skills

Rhythm

Chords

More

Folk & Country
Strum Pattern 1

Example of the above shown in TAB:

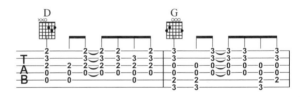

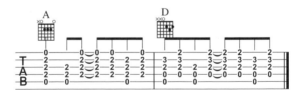

Note: the exact number of strings hit for each strum is down to taste.

Folk & Country
Strum Pattern 2

Basics

Folk

Blues

Rock
'n'Roll

Pop
Rock

Heavy
Rock

Alt.
Rock

Other
Styles

Skills

Rhythm

Chords

More

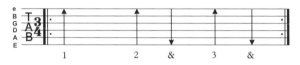

Note: can be played with straight or swung eighths.

An example of the above strum pattern is shown below in two variations (one bar each):

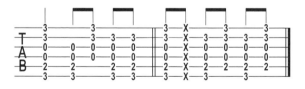

x = fret hand mute – will work better at faster tempos here.

Basics

Folk

Blues

Rock
'n'Roll

Pop
Rock

Heavy
Rock

Alt.
Rock

Other
Styles

Skills

Rhythm

Chords

More

Folk & Country
Strum Pattern 3

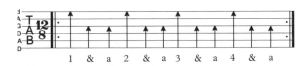

Example of the above with varied ending:

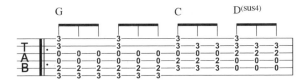

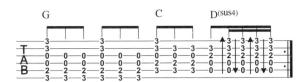

Folk & Country
Strum Pattern 4: 'Boom Chick' Folk or Country Style

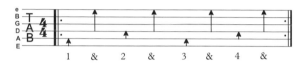

Example of the above with add9 and sus4 chords:

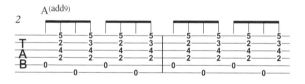

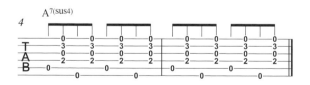

Basics

Folk

Blues

Rock 'n'Roll

Pop Rock

Heavy Rock

Alt. Rock

Other Styles

Skills

Rhythm

Chords

More

Basics

Folk

Blues

Rock
'n'Roll

Pop
Rock

Heavy
Rock

Alt.
Rock

Other
Styles

Skills

Rhythm

Chords

More

Folk & Country
Strum Pattern 5

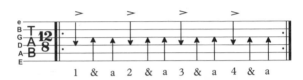

Note: mild upstrokes on upstrokes –'Celtic' variation.

Example of the above with extended chords for an open and more subtle sound:

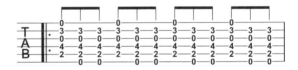

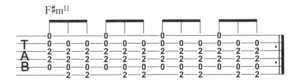

Strum Pattern 5 with Alternative Tuning

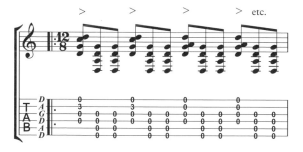

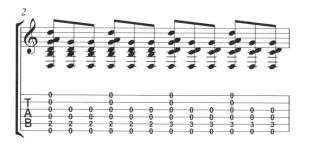

Basics

Folk

Blues

Rock 'n' Roll

Pop Rock

Heavy Rock

Alt. Rock

Other Styles

Skills

Rhythm

Chords

More

Basics

Folk

Blues

Rock 'n'Roll

Pop Rock

Heavy Rock

Alt. Rock

Other Styles

Skills

Rhythm

Chords

More

2

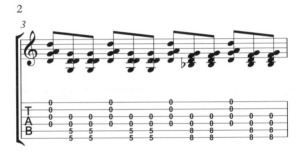

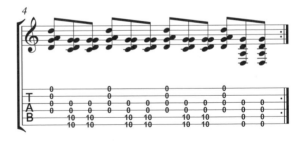

Folk & Country
Strum Pattern 6:
Bluegrass Rhythm

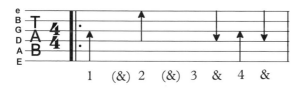

1 (&) 2 (&) 3 & 4 &

typically around 100 b.p.m.

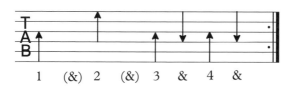

1 (&) 2 (&) 3 & 4 &

Basics
Folk
Blues
Rock 'n'Roll
Pop Rock
Heavy Rock
Alt. Rock
Other Styles
Skills
Rhythm
Chords
More

Folk & Country
Strum Pattern 6:
Notated Example

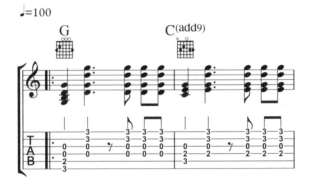

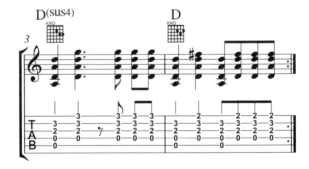

Folk & Country
Picking Pattern 1:
Basic Arpeggiated Picking

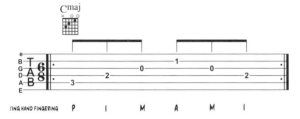

PICKING HAND FINGERING   P   I   M   A   M   I

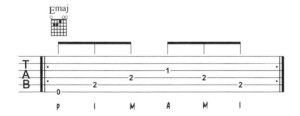

P   I   M   A   M   I

Basics

Folk

Blues

Rock 'n'Roll

Pop Rock

Heavy Rock

Alt. Rock

Other Styles

Skills

Rhythm

Chords

More

Folk & Country
Picking Pattern 2

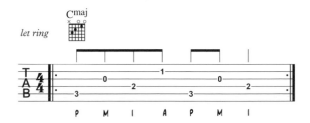

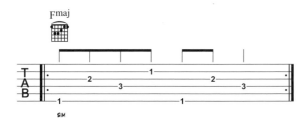

Folk & Country
Strum Pattern 3:
Basic Travis Picking

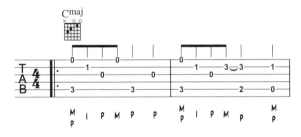

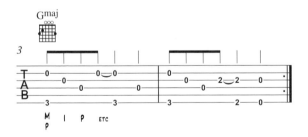

Basics

Folk

Blues

Rock 'n'Roll

Pop Rock

Heavy Rock

Alt. Rock

Other Styles

Skills

Rhythm

Chords

More

Basics

Folk

Blues

Rock
'n'Roll

Pop
Rock

Heavy
Rock

Alt.
Rock

Other
Styles

Skills

Rhythm

Chords

More

Folk & Country
Pattern 4: Basic 'Clawhammer' ('Bom-diddy' Rhythm)

A strum/pick hybrid: all downstrokes.
i, m and a strum or 'hammer' the strings, only p (thumb)
actually picks

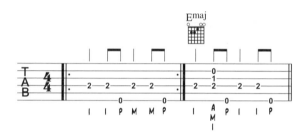

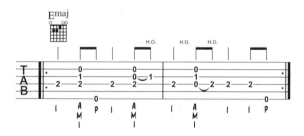

Here are a few useful chord diagrams for the examples in this chapter. Link to flametreemusic.com to see and hear a full range of chords:

Basics

Folk

Blues

Rock 'n' Roll

Pop Rock

Heavy Rock

Alt. Rock

Other Styles

Skills

Rhythm

Chords

More

C   C Major
1st (C), 3rd (E), 5th (G)

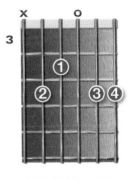

Cadd9   C Major add 9th
1st (C), 3rd (E), 5th (G), 9th (D)

D   D Major
1st (D), 3rd (F♯), 5th (A)

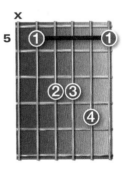

Dsus4   D Suspended 4th
1st (D), 4th (G), 5th (A)

Basics

Folk

Blues

Rock 'n'Roll

Pop Rock

Heavy Rock

Alt. Rock

Other Styles

Skills

Rhythm

Chords

More

E   E Major
1st (E), 3rd (G♯), 5th (B)

Em9   E Minor 9th
1st (E), ♭3rd (G), 5th (B),
♭7th (D), 9th (F♯)

F   F Major
1st (F), 3rd (A), 5th (C)

F♯m11   F♯ Minor 11th
1st (F♯), ♭3rd (A), 5th (C),
♭7th (E), 9th (G♯), 11th (B)

Folk & Country

Basics

Folk

Blues

Rock
'n'Roll

Pop
Rock

Heavy
Rock

Alt.
Rock

Other
Styles

Skills

Rhythm

Chords

More

G G Major
1st (G), 3rd (B), 5th (D)

A A Major
1st (A), 3rd (C#), 5th (E)

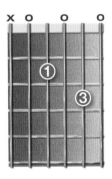

A7sus4 A Dominant 7th sus4
1st (A), 4th (D), 5th (E), ♭7th (G)

Aadd9 A Major add 9th
1st (A), 3rd (C#), 5th (E), 9th (B)

61

Basics

Folk

Blues

Rock
'n'Roll

Pop
Rock

Heavy
Rock

Alt.
Rock

Other
Styles

Skills

Rhythm

Chords

More

3

Blues, Soul & R'n'B

Many musical styles have their core in blues
music: without the blues, there would have
been no Beatles, Jimi Hendrix, Led Zeppelin,
James Brown, Stevie Wonder, or Oasis.
This chapter includes a range of blues strum
patterns and examples, including the
twelve-bar blues as well as soul and funk.

Basics

Folk

Blues

Rock
'n'Roll

Pop
Rock

Heavy
Rock

Alt.
Rock

Other
Styles

Skills

Rhythm

Chords

More

Basics

Folk

Blues

Rock
'n'Roll

Pop
Rock

Heavy
Rock

Alt.
Rock

Other
Styles

Skills

Rhythm

Chords

More

Blues Music

The blues has played a larger role in the history of popular music than any other genre. It is a direct ancestor to musical styles as diverse as rock'n'roll, rock, heavy metal, soul, funk and pop.

Playing the Blues

Blues is based around the blues scale (see opposite), which is a pentatonic minor scale with an added flat fifth note (the 'blue' note). Blues music is often played in the keys of A, D, E and G as they are all easy keys to play on the guitar. The style has an odd harmonic structure, as the blues scale is usually played or sung over chords that are all dominant sevenths (e.g. A7, D7 and E7 in the key of A) or chords derived from them.

There are two main blues styles: traditional acoustic blues and urban electric blues.

Guidance

Acoustic blues normally requires a 'finger-style' approach, in which the thumb of the right hand – assuming the player is right-handed – plays a steady bass-note groove while the melody or licks are picked out by the first and second fingers. Most of this is performed quite forcefully, although acoustic blues players rest the side of their picking hand across the strings at times to make sure the bass notes don't ring out too loudly.

Basics

Folk

Blues

Rock 'n'Roll

Pop Rock

Heavy Rock

Alt. Rock

Other Styles

Skills

Rhythm

Chords

More

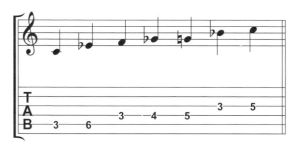

ABOVE: C Blues Scale

Basics

Folk

Blues

Rock
'n'Roll

Pop
Rock

Heavy
Rock

Alt.
Rock

Other
Styles

Skills

Rhythm

Chords

More

Playing Electric Blues

Urban electric blues guitar is usually played within the context of a band, so it is normally restricted to lead or rhythm playing at any one time. Some electric guitar players use a plectrum (pick) to achieve better articulation, while others favour a more earthy finger-style approach.

Blues Slide Effect

You can produce a blues slide effect by playing a note on a string and, while holding the string firmly down, slide along the fingerboard to another note. You can even slide across two or more strings at a time by barring your fretting finger across the strings and moving it along the neck in the same way. To obtain a vibrato effect, play a fretted note and move the string from side to side – across the fingerboard – with your fretting finger. This makes a sustained note sound more expressive or even aggressive.

The Twelve-Bar Blues

Tens of thousands of blues songs are based around
the most common chord progression in the history
of popular music: the twelve-bar blues sequence.

This can take various forms, but always uses
the 'I', 'IV' and 'V' of a key, where the roman
numerals in capitals refer to major triads formed
from the key's scale. In C, these would be the
chord C (I), F (IV), and G (V). It's common to
use sevenths in these chords too. An example of a
twelve-bar progression using these chords is below:

|| C7 | C7 | C7 | C7 |

| F7 | F7 | C7 | C7 |

| G7 | F7 | C7 | G7 :||

Basics

Folk

Blues

Rock
'n'Roll

Pop
Rock

Heavy
Rock

Alt.
Rock

Other
Styles

Skills

Rhythm

Chords

More

Basics

Folk

Blues

Rock
'n'Roll

Pop
Rock

Heavy
Rock

Alt.
Rock

Other
Styles

Skills

Rhythm

Chords

More

Soul

Soul music emerged from rhythm and blues (R&B) during the 1950s, and Ray Charles is widely acknowledged to be the first soul star. Blind from the age of six, Charles became interested in gospel and blues music, and developed a unique singing and songwriting style. Soul artists that followed included Otis Redding, Jackie Wilson and Aretha Franklin. By the mid-1960s Motown had been established in Detroit, with artists such as Smokey Robinson, the Supremes, the Four Tops, Marvin Gaye and Stevie Wonder.

Funk

Funk also emerged out of R&B and soul during the 1960s, when artists such as James Brown and his guitarist Jimmy Nolen developed a rhythm style so powerful that the melody and harmony were forced to take a back seat. It was popularized even further

Basics

Folk

Blues

Rock 'n'Roll

Pop Rock

Heavy Rock

Alt. Rock

Other Styles

Skills

Rhythm

Chords

More

during the 1970s by acts such as the Isley Brothers, Earth Wind & Fire, Funkadelic and Chic.

Playing Soul Guitar

Although soul and funk are both played by electric guitarists, the styles are different. Soul guitar is usually simple guitar chords or repetitive licks that fit in with a groove but don't interfere with the vocals. Funk guitar is usually a series of short licks that form a part of the groove upon which the song is based. These syncopated licks, along with the bass line, give the tune a funk 'edge'.

Playing Funk Guitar

The rhythmic way you play the guitar is key in achieving a funky sound.

Funk guitar tends to be played on treble strings and away from the chord root notes, as the bass

Basics

Folk

Blues

Rock
'n'Roll

Pop
Rock

Heavy
Rock

Alt.
Rock

Other
Styles

Skills

Rhythm

Chords

More

player usually has the job of playing these. Funk guitarists often play extended chords such as ninths, minor ninths and 11ths to give the groove an almost jazzy feel. Guitarists usually play these chords with simple shapes that can be moved all around the guitar neck.

Another funk technique uses rhythmic strumming on strings muted by the fretting hand, alternated with ringing extended chords or simple licks. An example that features this type of style is Isaac Hayes' 'Shaft' (1971), which famously also uses a wah-wah effect.

See pages 83–87 for some soul and funk strum patterns and examples. To start with though, there are a number of Blues patterns and examples to try, from a jump blues to a 'texas shuffle' style. Opposite is a reminder of common symbols that you may come across in some of the examples in this chapter.

Useful Symbols

Basics

Folk

Blues

Rock 'n'Roll

Pop Rock

Heavy Rock

Alt. Rock

Other Styles

Skills

Rhythm

Chords

More

Upstrum: V

Upstrum on TAB: ↑

Downstrum: ⊓

Downstrum on TAB: ↓

Time Signatures (examples):   4/4, 3/4, 6/8

Repeat signs: ‖: :‖

Accent: >

Slide (ascending):   ⟋

Slide (descending):   ⟍

Mute: X

Palm Mute: P.M.

Hammer-On: H.O.

Staccato: ♪

Basics

Folk

Blues

Rock
'n'Roll

Pop
Rock

Heavy
Rock

Alt.
Rock

Other
Styles

Skills

Rhythm

Chords

More

Blues
Strum Pattern 1

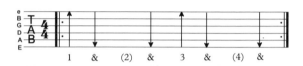

Mute strings with strumming hand on beats 2 and 4. The first note in every beat (first 8th note) is longer in duration than the second one each time.

Strum Pattern 2

Muted Shuffle.
Same time feel: uneven eighths.

Strum Pattern 3

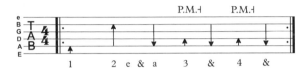

Pattern 3 on an E7 chord:

Basics

Folk

Blues

Rock
'n'Roll

Pop
Rock

Heavy
Rock

Alt.
Rock

Other
Styles

Skills

Rhythm

Chords

More

Basics

Folk

Blues

Rock
'n'Roll

Pop
Rock

Heavy
Rock

Alt.
Rock

Other
Styles

Skills

Rhythm

Chords

More

Blues
Strum Pattern 4:
Jump Blues

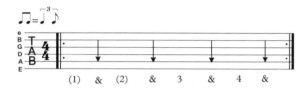

This is a strumming pattern in a Blues/R'n'B style: Jump blues off-beats.

A notated example is shown opposite, running onto the next two pages.

Pattern 4:
Notated Example

Basics

Folk

Blues

Rock
'n'Roll

Pop
Rock

Heavy
Rock

Alt.
Rock

Other
Styles

Skills

Rhythm

Chords

More

Basics

Folk

Blues

Rock
'n'Roll

Pop
Rock

Heavy
Rock

Alt.
Rock

Other
Styles

Skills

Rhythm

Chords

More

2

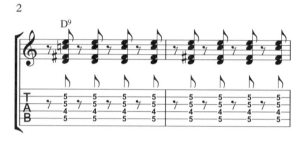

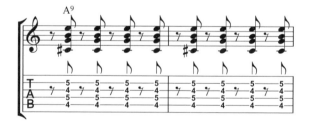

3

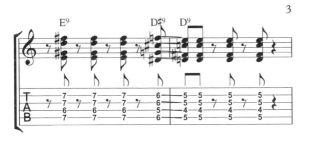

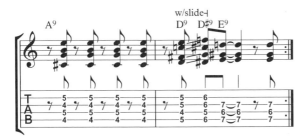

Basics

Folk

Blues

Rock
'n'Roll

Pop
Rock

Heavy
Rock

Alt.
Rock

Other
Styles

Skills

Rhythm

Chords

More

Basics

Folk

Blues

Rock
'n'Roll

Pop
Rock

Heavy
Rock

Alt.
Rock

Other
Styles

Skills

Rhythm

Chords

More

Blues
Strum Pattern 5
'Texas' Shuffle Part 1

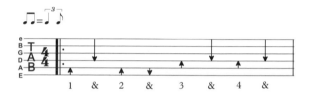

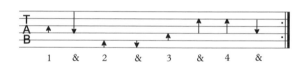

String combinations are chord-specific – this
example works on a chord with its root on the
6th string (see notated example of a blues in E
on pages 80–82)

Basics

Folk

Blues

Rock
'n'Roll

Pop
Rock

Heavy
Rock

Alt.
Rock

Other
Styles

Skills

Rhythm

Chords

More

Blues
Strum Pattern 5
'Texas' Shuffle Part 2

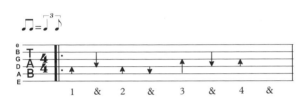

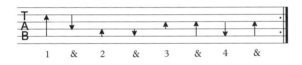

String combinations are chord-specific – this
example works on a chord with its root on
the 5th string (see notated example on
pages 80–82)

Basics

Folk

Blues

Rock
'n'Roll

Pop
Rock

Heavy
Rock

Alt.
Rock

Other
Styles

Skills

Rhythm

Chords

More

Pattern 5:
Notated Example

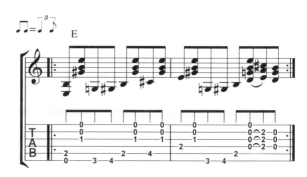

E

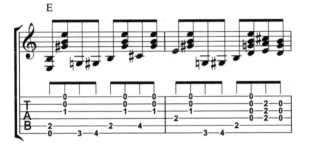

B⁷   A

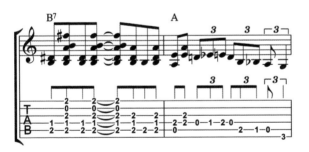

Basics

Folk

Blues

Rock
'n'Roll

Pop
Rock

Heavy
Rock

Alt.
Rock

Other
Styles

Skills

Rhythm

Chords

More

This notated example, which uses the pattern from pages 78–79 as its basis, includes the chords of E, A and B7. Chord diagrams for these can be found in the chord reference section at the end of this section, on pages 88–91.

Soul/Funk/Disco
Strum Pattern

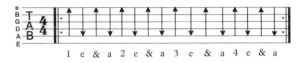

The above shows the direction of strum.

The below version shows the fretting hand
muting (remember: x signifies mute).

A notated example is shown on the following
page (again, x signifies mute).

Basics

Folk

Blues

Rock
'n'Roll

Pop
Rock

Heavy
Rock

Alt.
Rock

Other
Styles

Skills

Rhythm

Chords

More

Soul/Funk/Disco
Pattern: Notated Version

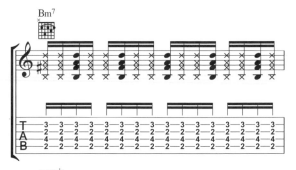

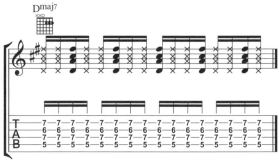

Funk
Strum Pattern 1

1 e & a 2 e & a 3 e & a 4 e & a

Basics

Folk

Blues

Rock 'n' Roll

Pop Rock

Heavy Rock

Alt. Rock

Other Styles

Skills

Rhythm

Chords

More

A notated version is given on the next page, showing a typical late 1970s funk guitar part. The time feel is swung 16th notes. Note the more complex pattern of ghost notes compared to the disco-related pattern shown on pages 83–84.

On page 87, there is a 1990s hip-hop influenced funk example, which should be played with swung 1/16ths, with a laid back feel around ♪=85. In that example, strum downbeats (1, 2, 3, 4) and '&'s downwards – 'e's' and 'a's' upwards. Chord symbols are included for analysis only.

Funk
Strum Pattern 1:
Notated Version

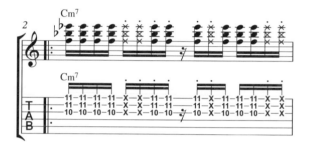

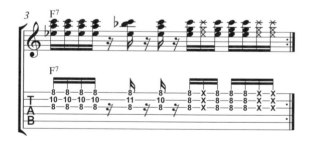

Basics

Folk

Blues

Rock 'n'Roll

Pop Rock

Heavy Rock

Alt. Rock

Other Styles

Skills

Rhythm

Chords

More

Funk
Strum Pattern 2

Basics

Folk

Blues

Rock 'n'Roll

Pop Rock

Heavy Rock

Alt. Rock

Other Styles

Skills

Rhythm

Chords

More

Here are a few useful chord diagrams for the examples in this chapter. Link to flametreemusic.com to see and hear a full range of chords:

Cm7 C Minor 7th
1st (C), ♭3rd (E♭), 5th (G), ♭7th (B♭)

Dmaj7 D Major 7th
1st (D), 3rd (F♯), 5th (A), 7th (C♯)

D7   D Dominant 7th
1st (D), 3rd (F♯), 5th (A), ♭7th (C)

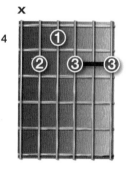

D9   D Dominant 9th
1st (D), 3rd (F♯),5th (A), ♭7th (C), 9th (E)

Basics

Folk

Blues

Rock
'n'Roll

Pop
Rock

Heavy
Rock

Alt.
Rock

Other
Styles

Skills

Rhythm

Chords

More

E♭9 E♭ Dominant 9th
1st (E♭), 3rd (G),
5th (B♭), ♭7th (D♭), 9th (F)

E E Major
1st (E), 3rd (G♯), 5th (B)

E7 E Dominant 7th
1st (E), 3rd (G♯),
5th (B), ♭7th (D)

E9 E Dominant 9th
1st (E), 3rd (G♯),
5th (B), ♭7th (D), 9th (F♯)

Guitar Strumming Patterns

Basics

Folk

Blues

Rock
'n'Roll

Pop
Rock

Heavy
Rock

Alt.
Rock

Other
Styles

Skills

Rhythm

Chords

More

F7   F Dominant 7th
1st (F), 3rd (A), 5th (C), ♭7th (E♭)

A   A Major
1st (A), 3rd (C♯),

Am   A Minor
1st (A), ♭3rd (C), 5th (E)

A9   A Dominant 9th
1st (A), 3rd (C♯),
5th (E), ♭7th (G), 9th (B)

B7   B Dominant 7th
1st (B), 3rd (D♯), 5th (F♯), ♭7th (A)

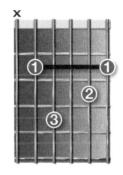

Bm7   B Minor 7th
1st (B), ♭3rd (D), 5th (F♯), ♭7th (A)

Basics
Folk
Blues
Rock 'n'Roll
Pop Rock
Heavy Rock
Alt. Rock
Other Styles
Skills
Rhythm
Chords
More

Basics

Folk

Blues

Rock
'n'Roll

Pop
Rock

Heavy
Rock

Alt.
Rock

Other
Styles

Skills

Rhythm

Chords

More

4

Rock'n'Roll

Born from the Blues, Country music and Rhythm and Blues, Rock'n'Roll was a popular style of music that evolved in the '50s. In this chapter you'll find three of its typical strumming patterns with examples of them in action. Also includes guidance on the types of chords used to recreate this catchy musical genre.

Basics

Folk

Blues

Rock 'n'Roll

Pop Rock

Heavy Rock

Alt. Rock

Other Styles

Skills

Rhythm

Chords

More

Basics

Folk

Blues

Rock
'n'Roll

Pop
Rock

Heavy
Rock

Alt.
Rock

Other
Styles

Skills

Rhythm

Chords

More

Rock'n'Roll Music

Chuck Berry, rock'n'roll's first true king,
dragged the blues into an electric era that filled
the dancehalls with loud and joyful music.
Dramatically, in the 1950s the blues was thrust
together with a restless teenage generation and
created a demon child: rock'n'roll. At last, teenagers
could revel in a sound that reflected their rebellious,
hormonal angst.

Rock'n'roll would evolve into the broader genre
of rock in the following decade: it was the British
blues boom of the Sixties that secured the survival
of rock and blues with Jimmy Page, Eric Clapton,
Jeff Beck and Keith Richards transforming their
own love of the blues into a lasting musical form.

During the Rock'n'roll era there was also a surge in
the popularity of the electric guitar: the Gibson SG,
with its devil-horned silhouette, is a rock'n'roll icon.

Basics

Folk

Blues

Rock 'n'Roll

Pop Rock

Heavy Rock

Alt. Rock

Other Styles

Skills

Rhythm

Chords

More

Guidance

A common chord progression used in rock'n'roll
is the I IV V. This is also a common chord
progression in blues music (especially with dominant
sevenths), as the basis of the twelve-bar blues.

As discussed in the last chapter, the roman
numerals for 'I', 'IV' and 'V' refer to the first,
fourth and fifth major triads formed from a
key's scale.

In the key of C, this would be C, then F, then G.

In the key of D, this would be D, then G, then A.

In the key of E, this would be E, then A, then B.

In the key of G, this would be G, then C, then D.

In the key of A, this would be A, then D, then E.

Basics

Folk

Blues

Rock
'n'Roll

Pop
Rock

Heavy
Rock

Alt.
Rock

Other
Styles

Skills

Rhythm

Chords

More

Presented as a simple chord chart, and assuming standard 4/4 timing with four beats per bar, the progression in C could be notated as:

| C / / / |
| F / / / |
| G / / / |

A few of the examples in this chapter use the I IV V progression, and you can see pages 108–109 for some useful chord diagrams.

For more information on Chord Progressions see pages 364–369.

The table on page 98 is a reminder of common symbols that you may come across in the patterns and examples in this section.

Basics

Folk

Blues

Rock 'n'Roll

Pop Rock

Heavy Rock

Alt. Rock

Other Styles

Skills

Rhythm

Chords

More

Basics

Folk

Blues

Rock
'n'Roll

Pop
Rock

Heavy
Rock

Alt.
Rock

Other
Styles

Skills

Rhythm

Chords

More

Useful Symbols

Upstrum:	V
Upstrum on TAB:	↑
Downstrum:	⊓
Downstrum on TAB:	↓
Time Signatures (examples):	4/4, 3/4, 6/8
Repeat signs:	‖: :‖
Accent:	>
Slide (ascending):	╱
Slide (descending):	╲
Mute:	X
Palm Mute:	P.M.
Hammer-On:	H.O.
Staccato:	♩

Rock'n'Roll
Strum Pattern 1

A basic rock'n'roll rhythm pattern with typical accentation.

Strum Pattern 1:
Notated Version

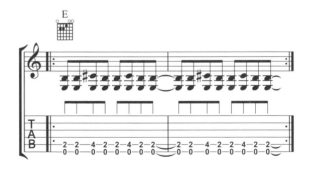

Basics

Folk

Blues

Rock 'n'Roll

Pop Rock

Heavy Rock

Alt. Rock

Other Styles

Skills

Rhythm

Chords

More

Basics

Folk

Blues

Rock 'n'Roll

Pop Rock

Heavy Rock

Alt. Rock

Other Styles

Skills

Rhythm

Chords

More

Rock'n'Roll
Strum Pattern 2

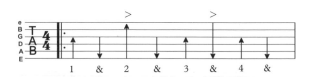

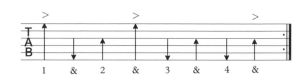

Another rock'n'roll rhythm pattern with typical accentation.

A notated version is shown opposite, running onto the next two pages.

Pattern 2:
Notated Version

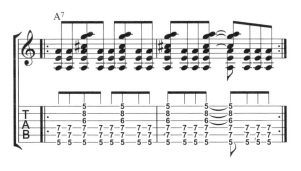

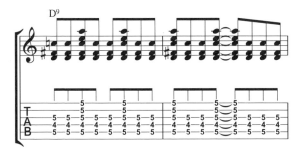

Basics

Folk

Blues

Rock 'n'Roll

Pop Rock

Heavy Rock

Alt. Rock

Other Styles

Skills

Rhythm

Chords

More

Basics

Folk

Blues

Rock 'n'Roll

Pop Rock

Heavy Rock

Alt. Rock

Other Styles

Skills

Rhythm

Chords

More

2

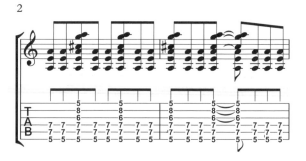

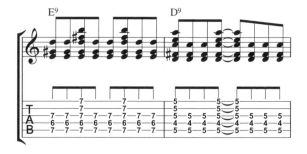

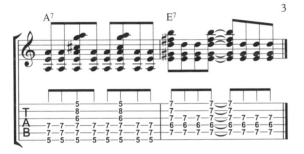

This notated example, which uses the pattern from page 100 as its basis, includes the chords of A7, D9, E9 and E7. Chord diagrams for these can be found in the chord reference section at the end of this section, on pages 108–109.

Basics

Folk

Blues

Rock 'n'Roll

Pop Rock

Heavy Rock

Alt. Rock

Other Styles

Skills

Rhythm

Chords

More

Basics

Folk

Blues

Rock 'n'Roll

Pop Rock

Heavy Rock

Alt. Rock

Other Styles

Skills

Rhythm

Chords

More

Rock'n'Roll
Strum Pattern 3

A third rock'n'roll rhythm pattern with suggested accents.

Dashed arrows indicate fretting hand mute.

A notated example on pages 105–107 is shown over a twelve-bar sequence.

Rock'n'Roll
Pattern 3: Notated Example

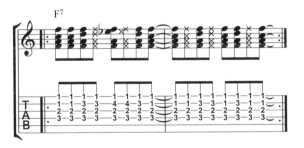

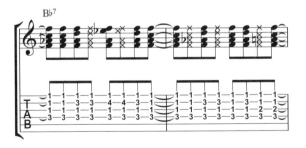

Basics

Folk

Blues

Rock
'n'Roll

Pop
Rock

Heavy
Rock

Alt.
Rock

Other
Styles

Skills

Rhythm

Chords

More

Basics

Folk

Blues

Rock
'n'Roll

Pop
Rock

Heavy
Rock

Alt.
Rock

Other
Styles

Skills

Rhythm

Chords

More

2

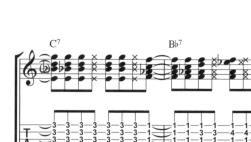

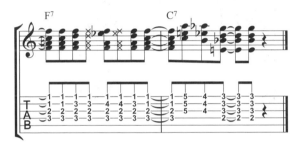

This notated example, which uses the pattern
from page 100 as its basis, includes the chords of
F7, B♭7 and C7. Chord diagrams for these can be
found in the chord reference section at the end of
this section, on pages 108–109.

Basics

Folk

Blues

Rock
'n'Roll

Pop
Rock

Heavy
Rock

Alt.
Rock

Other
Styles

Skills

Rhythm

Chords

More

Basics

Folk

Blues

Rock
'n'Roll

Pop
Rock

Heavy
Rock

Alt.
Rock

Other
Styles

Skills

Rhythm

Chords

More

Here are a few useful chord diagrams for the examples in this chapter. Link to flametreemusic.com to see and hear a full range of chords:

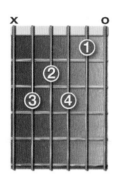

C7 C Dominant 7th
1st (C), 3rd (E), 5th (G), ♭7th (B♭)

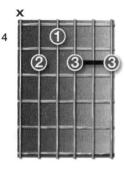

D9 D Dominant 9th
1st (D), 3rd (F♯), 5th (A),
♭7th (C), 9th (E)

E E Major
1st (E), 3rd (G♯), 5th (B)

E7 E Dominant 7th
1st (E), 3rd (G♯), 5th (B), ♭7th (D)

Basics

Folk

Blues

Rock 'n'Roll

Pop Rock

Heavy Rock

Alt. Rock

Other Styles

Skills

Rhythm

Chords

More

E9   E Dominant 9th
1st (E), 3rd (G#),
5th (B), ♭7th (D), 9th (F#).

F7   F Dominant 7th
1st (F), 3rd (A), 5th (C), ♭7th

A7   A Dominant 7th
1st (A), 3rd (C#), 5th (E), ♭7th (G)

B♭7   B♭ Dominant 7th
1st (B♭), 3rd (D), 5th (F), ♭7th (A♭)

Basics

Folk

Blues

Rock
'n'Roll

Pop
Rock

Heavy
Rock

Alt.
Rock

Other
Styles

Skills

Rhythm

Chords

More

5

Pop Rock

This chapter includes strumming patterns inspired by such artists as David Bowie, Iggy Pop and The Beatles. There are also several examples to try, shown using popular and simple chord sequences such as the I V vi IV progression. A couple of pages of useful chord diagrams follow the various strum patterns.

Basics

Folk

Blues

Rock 'n'Roll

Pop Rock

Heavy Rock

Alt. Rock

Other Styles

Skills

Rhythm

Chords

More

Basics

Folk

Blues

Rock
'n'Roll

Pop
Rock

Heavy
Rock

Alt.
Rock

Other
Styles

Skills

Rhythm

Chords

More

Pop Rock Music

The roots of rock's softer, smoother, more melodic sides veering into pop reach back to Hank Marvin's smooth, elegant lines in The Shadows of the early sixties.

More than a decade later this flowered into a succession of cracking guitarists who wore their riffs cloaked in smart, listener-friendly melodies. From the electro-pulse of U2's The Edge to the tasteful, almost folksy licks of Mark Knopfler, rock's rebelliousness was being subsumed into the mainstream.

In this chapter the strums and examples are inspired by some of pop's greatest icons, including The Beatles, Dire Straits, and David Bowie.

See page 130–131 for some useful chords, and page 115 for a reminder of common notation symbols.

Basics

Folk

Blues

Rock
'n'Roll

Pop
Rock

Heavy
Rock

Alt.
Rock

Other
Styles

Skills

Rhythm

Chords

More

Basics

Folk

Blues

Rock
'n'Roll

Pop
Rock

Heavy
Rock

Alt.
Rock

Other
Styles

Skills

Rhythm

Chords

More

Guidance

The first example in this chapter is a hybrid mix of strumming and picking. We have included below a reminder of the fingerpicking labels for reference.

In music notation for fingerpicking, each picking finger is identified by a letter:

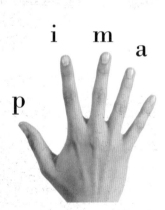

p = thumb

i = index finger

m = middle finger

a = ring finger

You can find further information on fingerpicking technique on pages 224–231, and details on strumming technique on pages 198–201.

Useful Symbols

Upstrum: V

Upstrum on TAB: ↑

Downstrum: ⊓

Downstrum on TAB: ↓

Time Signatures (examples):   **4/4, 3/4, 6/8**

Repeat signs: ‖: :‖

Accent: >

Slide (ascending):   ╱

Slide (descending):   ╲

Mute: X

Palm Mute: P.M.

Hammer-On: H.O.

Staccato: ♩.

Basics

Folk

Blues

Rock 'n'Roll

Pop Rock

Heavy Rock

Alt. Rock

Other Styles

Skills

Rhythm

Chords

More

115

Pop-Rock
Pick/Strum Hybrid Pattern:
Beatles-Style

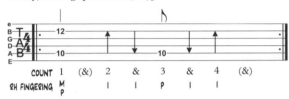

A full TAB version of the above pattern is shown below:

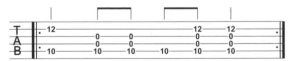

Pop-Rock
Pattern 2: Beatles-Style Acoustic Example

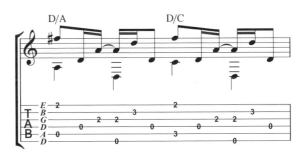

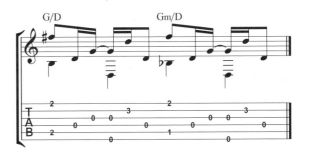

Basics

Folk

Blues

Rock 'n'Roll

Pop Rock

Heavy Rock

Alt. Rock

Other Styles

Skills

Rhythm

Chords

More

Pop-Rock
Notated Example

Another Beatles-inspired example – experiment with a capo to get as close as possible to the original.

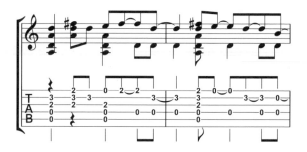

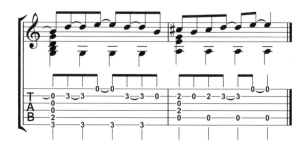

Pop-Rock
Strum Pattern 3
Early Beatles-Inspired
Accompaniment

Basics

Folk

Blues

Rock
'n'Roll

Pop
Rock

Heavy
Rock

Alt.
Rock

Other
Styles

Skills

Rhythm

Chords

More

TAB of above pattern with accents:

119

Basics

Folk

Blues

Rock
'n'Roll

Pop
Rock

Heavy
Rock

Alt.
Rock

Other
Styles

Skills

Rhythm

Chords

More

The example opposite uses the strumming pattern from page 119 as its basis.

It applies the pattern to a I V vi IV chord progression, in the key of C. This is a very common chord sequence in pop music, and in the key of C refers to the following chords:

C	G	Am	F
I	V	vi	IV
C major	G major	A minor	F major

On pages 124–125 you will find another popular chord progression applied to the strumming pattern on the pages before, inspired by David Bowie's 'Space Oddity'. In that example, the chord sequence is rearranged to I vi IV V. The example uses the key of G as its basis, so the sequence is then G, Em, C (with an added 9th), and D.

Pop-Rock
Example with
V vi IV Progression

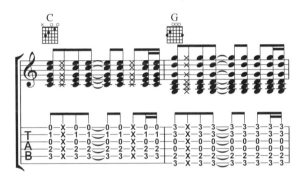

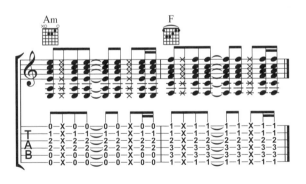

Basics

Folk

Blues

Rock
'n'Roll

Pop
Rock

Heavy
Rock

Alt.
Rock

Other
Styles

Skills

Rhythm

Chords

More

Basics

Folk

Blues

Rock
'n'Roll

Pop
Rock

Heavy
Rock

Alt.
Rock

Other
Styles

Skills

Rhythm

Chords

More

Pop-Rock
Strum Pattern 5

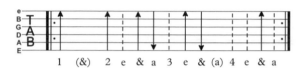

```
e ┌─────────────────────────────────────────┐
B─┬─║··                                   ··║
G─┤A║                                       ║
D─┤B║                                       ║
A─┴─║                                       ║
E   ║                                       ║
    1  (&)  2  e  &  a  3  e  &  (a) 4  e  &  a
```

This is a strum in the style of 'Space Oddity',
which works well at around ♪=75.

Dashed lines indicate either muted (ghost) notes
or a lighter strum, according to taste.

Shown opposite in full TAB.

Pattern 5:
Notated Version

Basics

Folk

Blues

Rock 'n'Roll

Pop Rock

Heavy Rock

Alt. Rock

Other Styles

Skills

Rhythm

Chords

More

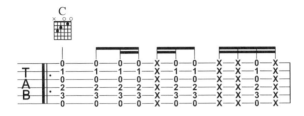

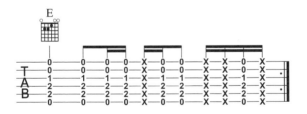

Basics

Folk

Blues

Rock 'n'Roll

Pop Rock

Heavy Rock

Alt. Rock

Other Styles

Skills

Rhythm

Chords

More

Pop-Rock
Example with I vi IV V Progression

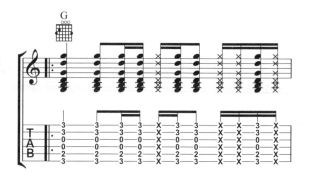

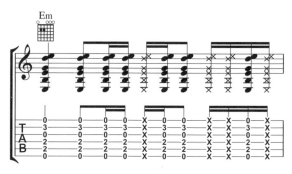

Basics

Folk

Blues

Rock
'n'Roll

Pop
Rock

Heavy
Rock

Alt.
Rock

Other
Styles

Skills

Rhythm

Chords

More

Strumming pattern for this example as per the
previous two pages. Works well at slower tempos
(e.g. ♪=80).

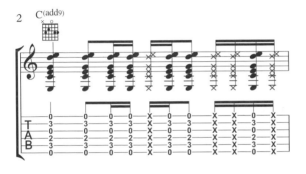

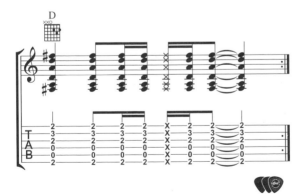

Basics

Folk

Blues

Rock
'n'Roll

Pop
Rock

Heavy
Rock

Alt.
Rock

Other
Styles

Skills

Rhythm

Chords

More

Pop-Rock
Strum Pattern 6

A strum in the style of 'Sultans of Swing'.

1 e & a 2 e & a 3 e & a 4 e & a

Suggested speed of ♪=130 – practise slowly and gradually work up to this approximate tempo.

A notated version is opposite – note the variation with ghost notes in bar 2.

Pattern 6:
Notated Version

Basics

Folk

Blues

Rock 'n'Roll

Pop Rock

Heavy Rock

Alt. Rock

Other Styles

Skills

Rhythm

Chords

More

Basics

Folk

Blues

Rock
'n'Roll

**Pop
Rock**

Heavy
Rock

Alt.
Rock

Other
Styles

Skills

Rhythm

Chords

More

Pop-Rock
Strum Pattern 7

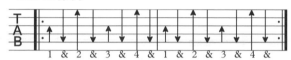

Shuffle feel $\sqcap = \overset{3}{\sqcap}$

```
T ||:          ↑              ↑              ↑              ↑     :||
A ||:  ↑      ↓   ↓      ↑   ↓      ↓   ↓      ↑   ↓      ↓   ↓   :||
B
       1  &  2  &  3  &  4  &  1  &  2  &  3  &  4  &
```

This strum pattern is in the style of 'The
Passenger' or 'The Train Song'.

'Passenger' is around 130b.p.m.; 'Train Song'
around 100b.p.m.. What they both have
in common is the time feel and the lack of
emphasis on the downbeat in the guitar part.

A notated version is shown opposite.

Pattern 7:
Notated Version

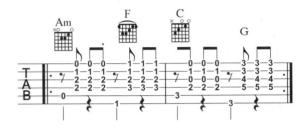

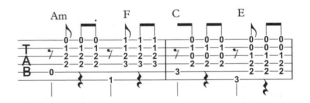

Basics

Folk

Blues

Rock 'n'Roll

Pop Rock

Heavy Rock

Alt. Rock

Other Styles

Skills

Rhythm

Chords

More

129

Here are a few useful chord diagrams for the examples in this chapter. Link to flametreemusic.com to see and hear a full range of chords:

C C Major
1st (C), 3rd (E), 5th (G)

Cadd9 C Major add 9th
1st (C), 3rd (E), 5th (G), 9th (D)

D D Major
1st (D), 3rd (F♯), 5th (A)

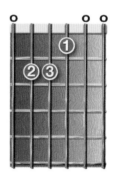

E E Major
1st (E), 3rd (G♯), 5th (B)

Em   E Minor
1st (E), ♭3rd (G), 5th (B)

F   F Major
1st (F), 3rd (A), 5th (C)

G   G Major
1st (G), 3rd (B), 5th (D)

Am   A Minor
1st (A), ♭3rd (C), 5th (E)

Basics

Folk

Blues

Rock 'n'Roll

Pop Rock

Heavy Rock

Alt. Rock

Other Styles

Skills

Rhythm

Chords

More

Basics

Folk

Blues

Rock
'n'Roll

Pop
Rock

Heavy
Rock

Alt.
Rock

Other
Styles

Skills

Rhythm

Chords

More

6

Metal, Prog & Heavy Rock

With roots in blues rock, hard rock and its developments into prog rock and heavy metal form a fascinating group of musical styles. This chapter begins with a few classic blues rock riffs to try, leading onto prog rock and heavy metal strum examples.

Basics

Folk

Blues

Rock 'n'Roll

Pop Rock

Heavy Rock

Alt. Rock

Other Styles

Skills

Rhythm

Chords

More

Basics

Folk

Blues

Rock 'n'Roll

Pop Rock

Heavy Rock

Alt. Rock

Other Styles

Skills

Rhythm

Chords

More

From Blues Rock to Heavy Metal

In the late Sixties and early Seventies, some artists were tiring of the pop-rock sounds and their bluesy roots. The new rock generations started to experiment with different musical traditions and the changes in recording and sound technology brought in new guitar pedal effects and loops.

Hard Rock

Hard rock guitar developed from and shares some of the characteristics of blues rock. The definition of hard rock can be a wide one, but the genre is generally accepted to have begun in the late Sixties when America's Frank Zappa, The Doors, Jimi Hendrix and Vanilla Fudge set the tone for the Seventies with distorted guitars, slowed-down, druggy riffs and extravagant stage presentation.

Basics

Folk

Blues

Rock
'n'Roll

Pop
Rock

**Heavy
Rock**

Alt.
Rock

Other
Styles

Skills

Rhythm

Chords

More

Heavy Metal

Although the term 'heavy metal' did not become
firmly established until the late 1970s, the roots for
this popular genre were firmly planted when Led
Zeppelin and Black Sabbath were formed a decade
earlier in the UK. While some artists loosened their
grip on their blues rock roots, Led Zeppelin hardened
the edges and toughened the core of their sound.

Prog Metal

The progressive movement of the Sixties and early
Seventies, exemplified by mostly British bands
like Pink Floyd, Yes, and (early) Genesis, came up
with music that largely relied on virtuosity for its
appeal, with shifting time signatures and complex
song structures. Progressive rock enjoyed a Nineties
revival which saw mostly American bands like
Dream Theater merge the complexities of the prog
genre with a harder-hitting, guitar-led edge.

Basics

Folk

Blues

Rock 'n'Roll

Pop Rock

Heavy Rock

Alt. Rock

Other Styles

Skills

Rhythm

Chords

More

Guidance

If you want to be a proficient rock guitarist, you'll need to know a variety of basic chord shapes.

Playing Rock

The most common open chords (ones that include open strings as well as fretted ones) are A, Am, B7, C, C7, D, Dm, D7, E, E7, F, G and G7, which will allow you to play songs in the popular rock keys of A, C, D, E and G.

Useful barre chords are the barred versions of the A and E shapes (major barre chords) and Am and Em shapes (minor barre chords). These will allow you to play in any key you want, as barre shapes can be played anywhere on the fingerboard.

Open chords are good for earthy strumming and would suit, for example, an Oasis-style song, while barre chords can be used to create a more powerful, aggressive sound for punk and hard-rock styles. Major chords are ideal for upbeat rock riffs, while minor ones are more suitable for ballads.

Strumming and Picking

Rhythmically, rock is fairly straightforward, with emphasis mainly on the first and third beats of the bar. Strumming is usually performed with downstrokes, as these supply more power, although more intricate rhythms might require alternating downstrokes and upstrokes. Many rock guitarists also play chords as arpeggios (playing all the separate notes in ascending or descending order) with a plectrum or the fingers of the picking hand, to produce a more melodious sound. This is used to great effect in rock classics such as Led Zeppelin's 'Stairway to Heaven' and the Animals' 'House of the Rising Sun'. Most rock solos feature the pentatonic minor and blues scales.

Basics

Folk

Blues

Rock 'n'Roll

Pop Rock

Heavy Rock

Alt. Rock

Other Styles

Skills

Rhythm

Chords

More

Basics

Folk

Blues

Rock
'n'Roll

Pop
Rock

Heavy
Rock

Alt.
Rock

Other
Styles

Skills

Rhythm

Chords

More

Playing Metal

Although most metal guitarists know a variety of chord shapes, you can play a lot of music in this style with power chords.

Power Chords

The most basic of these are two-note chords consisting of the first and fifth notes of the major scale, played on any two adjacent strings (such as the sixth and fifth strings) with your index finger fretting the root note (on the thicker string), and your third finger fretting the fifth note (on the lighter string) two frets further up the fingerboard. To play a G power chord on the sixth and fifth strings (E and A), for example, place your index finger behind the third fret on the sixth string and your third finger behind the fifth fret on the fifth string and then strum those strings only.

Basics

Folk

Blues

Rock 'n'Roll

Pop Rock

Heavy Rock

Alt. Rock

Other Styles

Skills

Rhythm

Chords

More

Add Power to Power Chords

You can strengthen your power chords further by adding an extra note, one that is an octave higher than your root note, on the next adjacent string. This is easy to do as it is in the same fret as the fifth interval note; to play a three-note G power chord on the sixth, fifth and fourth strings, adopt the fingering position already described, and place your fourth (little) finger behind the fifth fret on the fourth string to get that octave note. Bear in mind, though, that when you're playing any power chords, you should only strum the strings you are fretting.

The barred versions of the open A and E shapes and the open Am and Em shapes are useful here too, as they allow you to play full major or minor chords in any key you want, as the shapes can be used anywhere on the fingerboard. Diminished and augmented chords can also be useful for metal as they produce a dissonant, disturbing effect.

Basics

Folk

Blues

Rock
'n'Roll

Pop
Rock

Heavy
Rock

Alt.
Rock

Other
Styles

Skills

Rhythm

Chords

More

Getting in Rhythm

Rhythmically, metal is usually relentless, with emphasis on insistent eighth- or sixteenth-note rhythms and a heavy accent on the first and other beats. Strumming is usually performed with downstrokes as these supply more power, although more intricate rhythms will sometimes require alternating downstrokes and upstrokes. Metal guitarists also perform muted versions of their riffs by resting the side of their picking hand against the strings. This creates a great dynamic effect when combined with unmuted versions of the riffs.

Scale-wise, the pentatonic scales and all the common major scale modes are useful. If you want to play a thrash-related style you will have to learn to play them fast with alternate picking. If you want to get quicker results, practise hammer-ons and pull-offs, as these can easily be combined with picked notes to create rapid phrases within a solo.

Useful Symbols

Upstrum:	V
Upstrum on TAB:	↑
Downstrum:	⊓
Downstrum on TAB:	↓
Time Signatures (examples):	4/4, 3/4, 6/8
Repeat signs:	‖: :‖
Accent:	>
Slide (ascending):	╱
Slide (descending):	╲
Mute:	X
Palm Mute:	P.M.
Hammer-On:	H.O.
Staccato:	♩

Basics

Folk

Blues

Rock 'n'Roll

Pop Rock

Heavy Rock

Alt. Rock

Other Styles

Skills

Rhythm

Chords

More

Basics

Folk

Blues

Rock 'n' Roll

Pop Rock

Heavy Rock

Alt. Rock

Other Styles

Skills

Rhythm

Chords

More

Blues Rock
Riff 1

Riff 1:
Notated Version

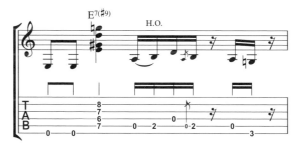

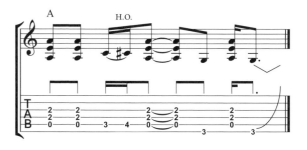

Basics

Folk

Blues

Rock
'n'Roll

Pop
Rock

**Heavy
Rock**

Alt.
Rock

Other
Styles

Skills

Rhythm

Chords

More

Basics

Folk

Blues

Rock
'n'Roll

Pop
Rock

Heavy
Rock

Alt.
Rock

Other
Styles

Skills

Rhythm

Chords

More

Blues Rock
Riff 2

Riff 2:
Notated Version

Basics

Folk

Blues

Rock 'n'Roll

Pop Rock

Heavy Rock

Alt. Rock

Other Styles

Skills

Rhythm

Chords

More

Basics

Folk

Blues

Rock 'n'Roll

Pop Rock

Heavy Rock

Alt. Rock

Other Styles

Skills

Rhythm

Chords

More

Opposite is a Prog Rock example inspired by Dream Theater.

The main technical issue with this example is not strumming, which can be done alternately downstroke followed by upstroke, but counting.

This can be done by tapping out the subdivisions, which can be kept at the same length and speed as the initial 16th notes in the first bar.

So there are 14 subdivisions in the 7/8 bars, 12 in the 3/4 bars, 6 in the 3/8 bar and 9 in the 9/16 bar, all taking up the same amount of time.

For tips on counting and keeping on top of timing, see the Rhythm chapter. Pages 310–313 deal specifically with understanding pulse, feeling the beat of the music, and handling trickier time signatures.

Prog Rock
Notated Example

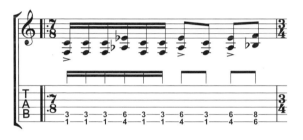

2

Basics

Folk

Blues

Rock
'n'Roll

Pop
Rock

**Heavy
Rock**

Alt.
Rock

Other
Styles

Skills

Rhythm

Chords

More

Heavy Metal
Strum Pattern:
Basic Gallop

(distorted electric guitar for all these examples)

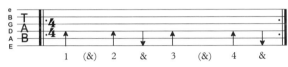

Variation with sustained chord:

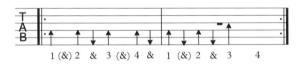

Example shown in TAB:

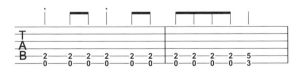

Basics

Folk

Blues

Rock 'n'Roll

Pop Rock

Heavy Rock

Alt. Rock

Other Styles

Skills

Rhythm

Chords

More

Further Variations

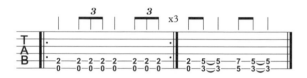

Heavy Metal
Notated Example

Showing use of rhythmic displacement. Experiment with both alternate picking and consecutive downstrokes. Slide between all double stops on adjacent frets.

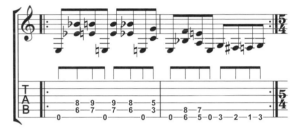

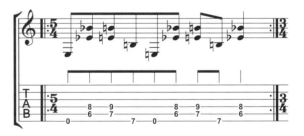

Basics

Folk

Blues

Rock 'n'Roll

Pop Rock

Heavy Rock

Alt. Rock

Other Styles

Skills

Rhythm

Chords

More

Basics

Folk

Blues

Rock 'n'Roll

Pop Rock

Heavy Rock

Alt. Rock

Other Styles

Skills

Rhythm

Chords

More

2

D.C. al fine

Here are a few useful chord diagrams for the examples in this chapter. Link to flametreemusic.com to see and hear a full range of chords:

Basics

Folk

Blues

Rock 'n'Roll

Pop Rock

Heavy Rock

Alt. Rock

Other Styles

Skills

Rhythm

Chords

More

E7♯9 E Dominant 7th ♯9
1s (E), 3rd (G♯), 5th (B),
♭7th (D), ♯9th (F×)

Gm G Minor
1st (G), ♭3rd (B♭), 5th (D)

Gm7 G Minor 7th
1st (G), ♭3rd (B♭), 5th (D), ♭7th (F)

A A Major
1st (A), 3rd (C♯), 5th (E)

Basics

Folk

Blues

Rock 'n'Roll

Pop Rock

Heavy Rock

Alt. Rock

Other Styles

Skills

Rhythm

Chords

More

7

Alternative Rock

Alternative rock music styles developed in response to the perceived elitism of mainstream progressive, metal and hard rock of the 1970s and 80s. It encompasses Indie rock, punk rock and grunge rock. Strum and picking pattern examples for all these can be found here, with information on the genres and guidance on how to play within them.

Basics

Folk

Blues

Rock 'n'Roll

Pop Rock

Heavy Rock

Alt. Rock

Other Styles

Skills

Rhythm

Chords

More

Basics

Folk

Blues

Rock
'n'Roll

Pop
Rock

Heavy
Rock

**Alt.
Rock**

Other
Styles

Skills

Rhythm

Chords

More

Alternative Rock

One of the most powerful aspects of rock music is its ability to create and recreate a constant rebellion against itself. The punk explosion of the Seventies saw The Sex Pistols rip through TV screens and singles charts, opening the door to successive generations of simple, direct challenges to the royalties of rock. For some, like Radiohead or My Bloody Valentine, the rebellion is expressed through a rejection of lead-guitar breaks and melodies; for others it's the blistering capture of retro rock, like Jack White in The White Stripes, or Graham Coxon's gobby rhythm chops on his post-Blur solo albums. As the Eighties turned into the Nineties, a rush of loud, raw music emanated from across the northwest of the USA, bands like the Pixies and the Red Hot Chili Peppers ushering in the 'grunge' era. Nirvana guitarist and songwriter, Kurt Cobain, penned songs that combined urgency and noise with incredibly catchy melodies.

Basics

Folk

Blues

Rock
'n'Roll

Pop
Rock

Heavy
Rock

**Alt.
Rock**

Other
Styles

Skills

Rhythm

Chords

More

Punk

In 1976, punk suddenly appeared and bands
like the Sex Pistols, the Clash and the Damned
introduced a basic rock style that relied more on
attitude than technique.

However, it was a short-lived trend and by the late
1970s rock began to fragment into a number of
sub-genres, including new wave (an offshoot from
punk), stadium rock (the likes of Bruce Springsteen
and Queen) and the various strands of heavy metal
that were beginning to develop in the US and UK.

Indie

The Smiths were the dominant British 'indie' rock
band of the 1980s, and this was mainly down to
the unique combination of singer Morrissey's forlorn
crooning and the uncluttered rhythm guitar work
of Johnny Marr. They recorded a number of hit

Basics

Folk

Blues

Rock
'n'Roll

Pop
Rock

Heavy
Rock

**Alt.
Rock**

Other
Styles

Skills

Rhythm

Chords

More

singles and albums that laid down the foundations for the next generation of British guitar bands. R.E.M also boasted a unique singer/guitarist combination – Michael Stipe's cryptic vocals and the ringing guitar hooks of Peter Buck captivated millions before the group disbanded in 2011.

Grunge

Despite the influx of fresh indie bands into the album and singles charts during the 1980s, most of the popular bands from this period, including Bon Jovi and Guns N' Roses, were purveyors of straight-ahead rock. By the end of the decade, however, grunge – a vibrant mixture of punk and heavy metal – became a prominent movement with Nirvana, a Seattle-based band, at the helm.

Nirvana's success was down to a combination of strong material, stop-start dynamics, and the manic intensity of singer-guitarist Kurt Cobain.

Guidance

Chords in grunge rhythm playing are largely played
as fifth chords in order to achieve a controlled,
tighter sound.

Power Chords

Such two-note chords are known as 'power chords'.
These were covered in the section for playing Metal
earlier in this book, but are described again here for
ease of reference: basic versions consist of the first
and fifth notes of the major scale, played on any
two adjacent strings (such as the sixth and fifth
strings, or fourth and third strings) with your index
finger fretting the root note (on the thicker string)
and your third finger fretting the fifth note (on the
lighter string) two frets further up the fingerboard.

To play an A power chord on the sixth and fifth
strings (E and A strings), for example, place your

Basics

Folk

Blues

Rock
'n'Roll

Pop
Rock

Heavy
Rock

Alt.
Rock

Other
Styles

Skills

Rhythm

Chords

More

Basics

Folk

Blues

Rock
'n'Roll

Pop
Rock

Heavy
Rock

**Alt.
Rock**

Other
Styles

Skills

Rhythm

Chords

More

index finger behind the fifth fret on the sixth string
and your third finger behind the seventh fret on the
fifth string and then strum those strings only.

See the below notated example of power chords.

Useful Symbols

Upstrum: V

Upstrum on TAB: ↑

Downstrum: ⊓

Downstrum on TAB: ↓

Time Signatures (examples):   4/4, 3/4, 6/8

Repeat signs: ‖: :‖

Accent: >

Slide (ascending):   ╱

Slide (descending):   ╲

Mute: X

Palm Mute: P.M.

Hammer-On: H.O.

Staccato: ♩

Indie Rock
Strum Pattern 1

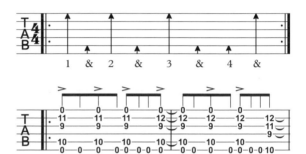

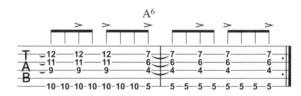

This 90s Indie Rock example uses some unusual chords based on a song by Jeff Buckley. All strums are downstrokes. The fourth string has to be muted with the fretting hand.

Indie Rock
Example 2

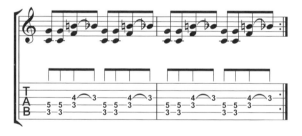

This is based on the first section of the chorus of a
Blur song. Can be strummed with alternating pick
strokes, or played with constant down strokes. The
fretting hand must mute the unplayed strings.

Basics

Folk

Blues

Rock
'n'Roll

Pop
Rock

Heavy
Rock

Alt.
Rock

Other
Styles

Skills

Rhythm

Chords

More

Basics

Folk

Blues

Rock
'n'Roll

Pop
Rock

Heavy
Rock

Alt.
Rock

Other
Styles

Skills

Rhythm

Chords

More

Punk
Example 1

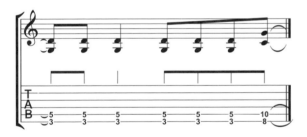

Distorted electric guitar.

Alternate strum as indicated. Keep the hand movement going when the note is held.

Punk
Strum Pattern 2

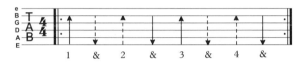

```
e
B   T  4
G   A  4
D   B
E
    1   &   2   &   3   &   4   &
```

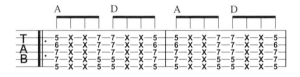

```
    A       D       A       D
T  5—X—X—7—7—X—X—5   5—X—X—7—7—X—X—5
A  6—X—X—7—7—X—X—6   6—X—X—7—7—X—X—6
B  7—X—X—7—7—X—X—7   7—X—X—7—7—X—X—7
   7—X—X—5—5—X—X—7   7—X—X—5—5—X—X—7
   5—X—X—5—5—X—X—5   5—X—X—5—5—X—X—5
```

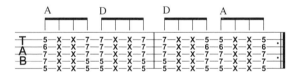

```
    A       D       D       A
T  5—X—X—7—7—X—X—7   7—X—X—5—5—X—X—5
A  6—X—X—7—7—X—X—7   7—X—X—6—6—X—X—6
B  7—X—X—7—7—X—X—7   7—X—X—7—7—X—X—7
   7—X—X—5—5—X—X—5   5—X—X—7—7—X—X—7
   5—X—X—5—5—X—X—5   5—X—X—5—5—X—X—5
```

Dashed lines on arrows indicate an instruction
to relax the fretting hand for a muted strum.

Navigation sidebar
Basics · Folk · Blues · Rock 'n'Roll · Pop Rock · Heavy Rock · Alt. Rock · Other Styles · Skills · Rhythm · Chords · More

Basics

Folk

Blues

Rock
'n'Roll

Pop
Rock

Heavy
Rock

**Alt.
Rock**

Other
Styles

Skills

Rhythm

Chords

More

The example opposite is based on an iconic grunge riff.

In it, the use of the treble strings is less important, as the emphasis is on the power chord, but the original artist often played all six.

In the original song it was played both with and without distortion, around ♪=105–110.

Kurt Cobain often started with an upwards strum, but you will achieve the same effect in a more natural-feeling way by starting on a downward strum.

Main divisions and 8ths will then fall as downstrokes.

Grunge
Riff

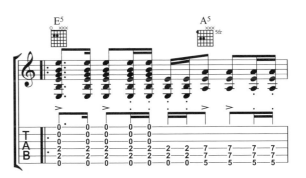

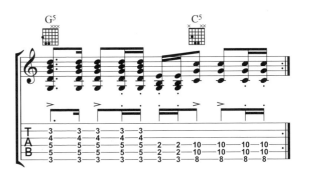

Basics

Folk

Blues

Rock 'n'Roll

Pop Rock

Heavy Rock

Alt. Rock

Other Styles

Skills

Rhythm

Chords

More

Indie Rock
Picking Pattern

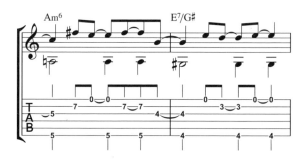

Basics

Folk

Blues

Rock
'n'Roll

Pop
Rock

Heavy
Rock

Alt.
Rock

Other
Styles

Skills

Rhythm

Chords

More

2

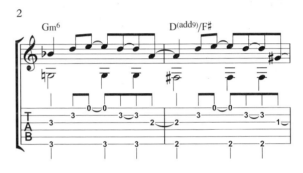

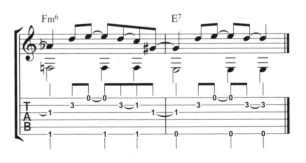

Basics

Folk

Blues

Rock 'n'Roll

Pop Rock

Heavy Rock

Alt. Rock

Other Styles

Skills

Rhythm

Chords

More

Basics

Folk

Blues

Rock
'n'Roll

Pop
Rock

Heavy
Rock

Alt.
Rock

Other
Styles

Skills

Rhythm

Chords

More

Here are a few useful chord diagrams for the
examples in this chapter. Link to flametreemusic.com
to see and hear a full range of chords:

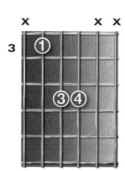

C5 C 5th (Power Chord)
1st (C), 5th (G)

D D Major
1st (D), 3rd (F♯), 5th (A)

D6 D Major 6th
1st (D), 3rd (F♯), 5th (A), 6th (B)

Em E Minor
1st (E), ♭3rd (G), 5th (B)

Basics

Folk

Blues

Rock
'n'Roll

Pop
Rock

Heavy
Rock

Alt.
Rock

Other
Styles

Skills

Rhythm

Chords

More

E° E Diminished Triad
1st (E), ♭3rd (G), ♭5th (B♭)

Em6 E Minor 6th
1st (E), ♭3rd (G), 5th (B), 6th (C♯)

E7 E Dominant 7th
1st (E), 3rd (G♯),
5th (B), ♭7th (D)

Fm6 F Minor 6th
1st (F), ♭3rd (A♭),
5th (C), 6th (D)

Basics

Folk

Blues

Rock 'n'Roll

Pop Rock

Heavy Rock

Alt. Rock

Other Styles

Skills

Rhythm

Chords

More

G5   G 5th (Power Chord)
1st (G), 5th (D)

Gm6   G Minor 6th
1st (G), ♭3rd (B♭), 5th (D), 6th (E)

A   A Major
1st (A), 3rd (C♯), 5th (E)

A5   A 5th (Power Chord)
1st (A), 5th (E)

Basics

Folk

Blues

Rock 'n'Roll

Pop Rock

Heavy Rock

Alt. Rock

Other Styles

Skills

Rhythm

Chords

More

A6 A Major 6th
1st (A), 3rd (C♯), 5th (E), 6th (F♯)

Am6 A Minor 6th
1st (A), ♭3rd (C), 5th (E), 6th (F♯)

B5 B 5th (Power Chord)
1st (B), 5th (F♯)

Bm11 B Minor 11th
1st (B), ♭3rd (D), 5th (F♯), ♭7th (A),
9th (C♯), 11th (E)

Basics

Folk

Blues

Rock
'n'Roll

Pop
Rock

Heavy
Rock

Alt.
Rock

Other
Styles

Skills

Rhythm

Chords

More

8

Other Styles

This chapter includes strumming patterns and examples for several additional musical styles you may want to try: from samba to reggae. Also includes a few swing styles, including the charleston. Each pattern is accompanied by an example of it in use, with guidance on how it can be played.

Basics

Folk

Blues

Rock 'n'Roll

Pop Rock

Heavy Rock

Alt. Rock

Other Styles

Skills

Rhythm

Chords

More

Basics

Folk

Blues

Rock
'n'Roll

Pop
Rock

Heavy
Rock

Alt.
Rock

**Other
Styles**

Skills

Rhythm

Chords

More

Samba, Reggae, Swing

The Samba

The samba is a hugely popular Afro-Brazilian rhythm. A well-known dance rhythm, the samba is upbeat and associated with parties and celebrations. It is heavily featured at the annual Rio de Janeiro carnivals and has been employed by artists as diverse as Samba-Rock band Trio Mocoto, fusion guitarist Pat Metheny and prog-rock keyboardist Patrick Moraz. Samba rhythms have also featured in many pop hits during the past 40 years.

Reggae

Reggae is a Jamaican style of music characterized by four beats to the measure with the off-beats (beats two and four) strongly accented. It evolved from ska, a music style born in the early 1960s

176

Basics

Folk

Blues

Rock
'n'Roll

Pop
Rock

Heavy
Rock

Alt.
Rock

Other
Styles

Skills

Rhythm

Chords

More

when Jamaican musicians changed the emphasis of the basic R&B rhythm from the first and third beats in the measure to the second and fourth.

Ska

The most influential ska group was the Skatalites. They adopted a tight, disciplined and steady rhythm, designed to whip the dancers into a frenzy.

Rocksteady

During the late 1960s, producers slowed the beat down to create a more soulful, laid-back reggae style called rocksteady. The main exponents of this style included Desmond Dekker and Jimmy Cliff.

Roots

Roots reggae introduced an even more laid-back rhythm with a prominent bass line in the 1970s. Eric Clapton's cover of Bob Marley's 'I Shot The Sheriff' (1974) helped to introduce the style to the world, and Marley later became a megastar.

Basics

Folk

Blues

Rock
'n'Roll

Pop
Rock

Heavy
Rock

Alt.
Rock

**Other
Styles**

Skills

Rhythm

Chords

More

Guidance

Reggae rhythm guitar is usually played as clean
'skanks' (downstrokes), with the strings damped
as soon as the chord is sounded, although double-
skank rhythms, where the downstrokes are swiftly
followed by upstrokes, are sometimes employed. The
chord progressions are simple; sometimes there are
only two chords in an entire song. There is rarely
any lead guitar in the style, although a second
guitarist will often play repetitive note phrases with
note damping (with the palm of the picking hand)
to enhance the groove.

You can use just about any electric solid-body
guitar and any reasonable amp to play reggae, but
you will probably want to keep the sound clean
and turn down your bass and mid-range controls.
Reggae rhythms can be very repetitive, so you
might want to use some effects pedals to create
more interest in the rhythm-guitar parts.

Useful Symbols

Upstrum:	V
Upstrum on TAB:	↑
Downstrum:	⊓
Downstrum on TAB:	↓
Time Signatures (examples):	4/4, 3/4, 6/8
Repeat signs:	‖: :‖
Accent:	>
Slide (ascending):	╱
Slide (descending):	╲
Mute:	X
Palm Mute:	P.M.
Hammer-On:	H.O.
Staccato:	♩

Basics

Folk

Blues

Rock 'n'Roll

Pop Rock

Heavy Rock

Alt. Rock

Other Styles

Skills

Rhythm

Chords

More

Basics

Folk

Blues

Rock
'n'Roll

Pop
Rock

Heavy
Rock

Alt.
Rock

**Other
Styles**

Skills

Rhythm

Chords

More

Samba
Strum Pattern 1

```
T ┌ │┃ ↑    ↑     ↑    ↑      ↑    ↑    ↑    ·┃
A   │┃                                        ┃
B   │┃ ↑        ↑        ↑       ↑           ·┃
    1 e & a  2 e & a  3 e  & a  4 e & a
```

Picking hand fingering: 5th or 6th string bass notes on downbeat use thumb (p). Use i, m and a for the 3-note chords.

There are many different possible variations and versions of samba rhythm playable on guitar. Many are played fingerstyle, which allows the guitar to take on some of the rhythmic roles of instruments (typically percussion) in a traditional samba band. Here is a basic, standard one – the notated version opposite includes a variation that would be played e.g. every 4 or 8 bars.

Pattern 1:
Notated Versions

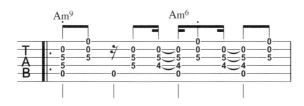

Basics

Folk

Blues

Rock
'n'Roll

Pop
Rock

Heavy
Rock

Alt.
Rock

**Other
Styles**

Skills

Rhythm

Chords

More

Basics

Folk

Blues

Rock
'n'Roll

Pop
Rock

Heavy
Rock

Alt.
Rock

Other
Styles

Skills

Rhythm

Chords

More

Samba
Strum Pattern 2

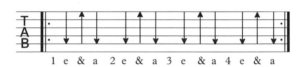

1 e & a 2 e & a 3 e & a 4 e & a

This one is a basic but authentic Samba accompaniment rhythm that works well played in the higher register on either an electric guitar or cavaquinho (a Brazilian instrument very similar to a ukulele). It could be played at the same time as the Samba Strum Pattern 1 is being played by another instrument.

Pattern 2:
Notated Version

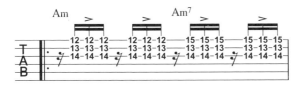

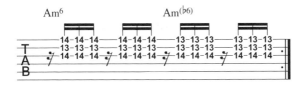

Basics

Folk

Blues

Rock 'n'Roll

Pop Rock

Heavy Rock

Alt. Rock

Other Styles

Skills

Rhythm

Chords

More

Basics

Folk

Blues

Rock 'n'Roll

Pop Rock

Heavy Rock

Alt. Rock

Other Styles

Skills

Rhythm

Chords

More

Reggae
Strum Pattern 1

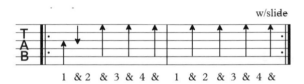

1 & 2 & 3 & 4 & 1 & 2 & 3 & 4 &

Ska in the style of 'Simmer Down', 'Freedom Sounds'.

N.B. using downstrokes tends to give more power and consistency to a 'skank' rhythm part such as this one.

Pattern 1:
Notated Version

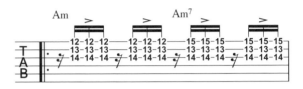

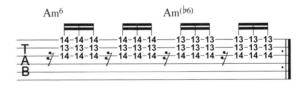

Basics

Folk

Blues

Rock 'n'Roll

Pop Rock

Heavy Rock

Alt. Rock

Other Styles

Skills

Rhythm

Chords

More

Basics

Folk

Blues

Rock
'n'Roll

Pop
Rock

Heavy
Rock

Alt.
Rock

Other
Styles

Skills

Rhythm

Chords

More

Reggae music is characterized by the emphasis on the off-beat, which pulls the tempo back and gives the music a laid-back feel.

Ska features a very simple bass on the beat with the keyboards and guitar bouncing off the beat. The resulting um-ska sound, which gave ska its name, is the basis for virtually all reggae styles that followed.

The pattern opposite works both at slower tempos (roots reggae) and uptempo (ska). On-beats are downward strums, and offbeats are upward.

Chords on beats 2 and 4 are muted every time; those on beats 1& and 3& are normal length and those on beats 2& and 4& are staccato.

186

Reggae
Strum Pattern 2

Basics

Folk

Blues

Rock
'n'Roll

Pop
Rock

Heavy
Rock

Alt.
Rock

Other
Styles

Skills

Rhythm

Chords

More

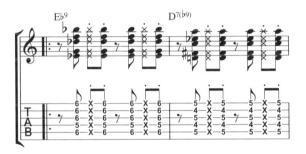

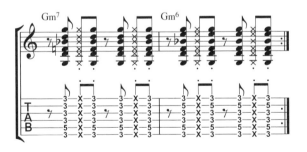

Basics

Folk

Blues

Rock
'n'Roll

Pop
Rock

Heavy
Rock

Alt.
Rock

Other
Styles

Skills

Rhythm

Chords

More

This example mainly uses the simplest swing rhythm, known as 'Charleston'.

The swing feel is attained by dividing each beat into two, then slightly lengthening the first division and shortening the second. Therefore, each on-beat strum can be played with a downstroke and each on-beat strum with a slightly delayed upstroke.

A rhythmic variation or 'fill' is included in bar 4.

For the example shown on page 190, the added staccatos are for guidance. Tied notes enable beats to be anticipated, giving a sense of forward movement and drive.

Each on-beat should be strummed with a downstroke; unused strings (e.g. the fifth, in many cases) can be muted with the fretting hand.

Swing
Strum Pattern 1

Basics

Folk

Blues

Rock
'n'Roll

Pop
Rock

Heavy
Rock

Alt.
Rock

**Other
Styles**

Skills

Rhythm

Chords

More

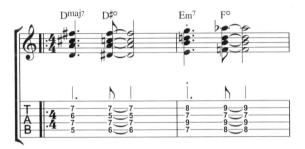

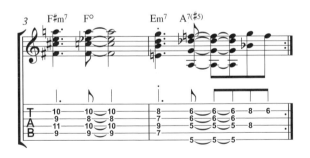

Swing
Strum Pattern 2

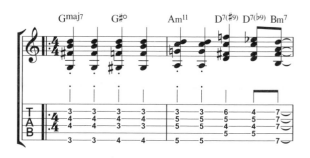

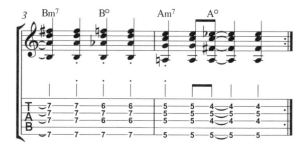

Basics
Folk
Blues
Rock 'n' Roll
Pop Rock
Heavy Rock
Alt. Rock
Other Styles
Skills
Rhythm
Chords
More

Here are a few useful chord diagrams for the examples in this chapter. Link to flametreemusic.com to see and hear a full range of chords:

Basics

Folk

Blues

Rock 'n'Roll

Pop Rock

Heavy Rock

Alt. Rock

Other Styles

Skills

Rhythm

Chords

More

Dmaj7 D Major 7th
1st (D), 3rd (F♯), 5th (A), 7th (C♯)

Em7 E Minor 7th
1st (E), ♭3rd (G), 5th (B), ♭7th (D)

F° F Diminished Triad
1st (F), ♭3rd (A♭), ♭5th (C♭)

Gm G Minor
1st (G), ♭3rd (B♭), 5th (D)

Basics

Folk

Blues

Rock 'n'Roll

Pop Rock

Heavy Rock

Alt. Rock

Other Styles

Skills

Rhythm

Chords

More

Gm6   G Minor 6th
1st (G), ♭3rd (B♭),
5th (D), 6th (E)

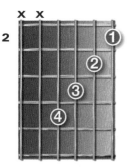

Gmaj7   G Major 7th
1st (G), 3rd (B), 5th (D),
7th (F#)

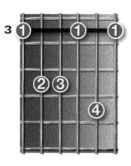

Gm7   G Minor 7th
1st (G), ♭3rd (B♭),
5th (D), ♭7th (F)

Am   A Minor
1st (A), ♭3rd (C), 5th (E)

A°   A Diminished Triad
1st (A), ♭3rd (C), ♭5th (E♭)

Am7   A Minor 7th
1st (A), ♭3rd (C), 5th (E), ♭7th (G)

B°   B Diminished Triad
1st (B), ♭3rd (D), ♭5th (F)

Bm7   B Minor 7th
1st (B), ♭3rd (D),
5th (F♯), ♭7th (A)

Basics

Folk

Blues

Rock 'n'Roll

Pop Rock

Heavy Rock

Alt. Rock

Other Styles

Skills

Rhythm

Chords

More

Basics

Folk

Blues

Rock
'n'Roll

Pop
Rock

Heavy
Rock

Alt.
Rock

Other
Styles

Skills

Rhythm

Chords

More

9

Skills

In order to play the previous patterns and examples, you may want to brush up on your guitar technique. Here you'll find advice on a number of basic techniques: from general strumming, fingerpicking and plectrum technique, to slides, string damping, using power chords for smooth chord changes, and alternative tunings.

Basics

Folk

Blues

Rock
'n'Roll

Pop
Rock

Heavy
Rock

Alt.
Rock

Other
Styles

Skills

Rhythm

Chords

More

Basics

Folk

Blues

Rock
'n'Roll

Pop
Rock

Heavy
Rock

Alt.
Rock

Other
Styles

Skills

Rhythm

Chords

More

Hand Position

If you don't position your hands in the optimum
way, learning strum and picking patterns might
prove difficult; playing with a good technique from
the start, by positioning your hands correctly, will
make learning new techniques relatively easy.

Picking Hand

1. If you're using a plectrum (pick), grip it
between the index (first) finger and the thumb.
Position the plectrum so that its tip extends
only just beyond the fingertip, by about ¼ in
(around 5 mm). Whilst this measurement
doesn't have to be exact, make sure that the
amount of plectrum that extends beyond
the index finger is not excessive: this would
result in a lack of pick control, making the
plectrum liable to flap around when striking the
strings – reducing both fluency and accuracy.

Basics

Folk

Blues

Rock
'n'Roll

Pop
Rock

Heavy
Rock

Alt.
Rock

Other
Styles

Skills

Rhythm

Chords

More

Alternatively, if you find that when you try to pick a string you often miss it completely, the cause is most likely to be not enough plectrum extending beyond the fingertip.

2. Although you need to hold the plectrum with a small amount of pressure so that it doesn't get knocked out of your hand when you strike the strings, be very careful not to grip the plectrum too tightly. Excessive gripping pressure can lead to muscular tension in the hand and arm, with a subsequent loss of flexibility and movement.

3. The most efficient way to pick single notes is to alternate between downstrokes and upstrokes. Unless you want to achieve a particular staccato sound, this 'alternate picking' technique should be used for all melodies or lead-guitar playing. For information on alternate picking, see pages 230–231, where you'll also find some picking exercises to try.

Basics

Folk

Blues

Rock
'n'Roll

Pop
Rock

Heavy
Rock

Alt.
Rock

Other
Styles

Skills

Rhythm

Chords

More

Strumming Technique

Strumming chords forms the foundation of any guitar player's range of techniques. Strumming can be used to accompany your own or someone else's singing; it can also be used to provide a backing for lead-guitar playing. Being able to strum in a variety of styles will enable you to play rhythm guitar in a wide range of musical genres.

Strum Technique

For the music to flow smoothly it's essential to develop a relaxed strumming action. It will aid the fluency of rhythm playing if the action comes from the wrist: a fluid and easy strumming action is best achieved this way, with the wrist loose and relaxed. If the wrist is stiff and not allowed to move freely then excessive arm movement will occur, as the strumming action will be forced to come from the elbow instead. As this can never move as fluently as the wrist, there will be a loss of smoothness and rhythmic potential.

Strumming Exercises

1. Begin by strumming an E minor chord using four downstrums per measure, and then experiment by inserting a quick upstrum between the second and third beats. The upstrum should be played by an upwards movement generated from the wrist, as

Basics

Folk

Blues

Rock
'n'Roll

Pop
Rock

Heavy
Rock

Alt.
Rock

Other
Styles

Skills

Rhythm

Chords

More

Basics

Folk

Blues

Rock 'n'Roll

Pop Rock

Heavy Rock

Alt. Rock

Other Styles

Skills

Rhythm

Chords

More

though the strumming hand is almost effortlessly bouncing back into position ready for the next downstrum. Keep practising this technique until it feels natural, always making sure that the arm itself isn't moving up and down when you're strumming.

2. Progress to adding two upstrums per bar: one between beats two and three, and one after the fourth beat. After the first two bars, try changing the chord to A minor and see if you

Basics

Folk

Blues

Rock
'n'Roll

Pop
Rock

Heavy
Rock

Alt.
Rock

Other
Styles

Skills

Rhythm

Chords

More

can keep the strumming pattern going. If you can't change the chord quickly enough then start again from the beginning, playing at a much slower tempo.

3. To really get the strumming hand moving try adding an upstrum after every downstrum. Although this strumming style would be too busy for most songs, this exercise does provide practice in building a fluent strumming technique. Make sure that you have the plectrum positioned correctly, with its tip extending only just beyond the index fingertip, so that it does not drag on the strings as you strum.

$\frac{4}{4}$ ‖   Em   ‖

```
■   V   ■   V   ■   V   ■   V
1   &   2   &   3   &   4   &
```

Basics

Folk

Blues

Rock 'n'Roll

Pop Rock

Heavy Rock

Alt. Rock

Other Styles

Skills

Rhythm

Chords

More

Playing Chords

Playing with a loose wrist action is an essential ingredient of developing a good strumming technique. Keeping the wrist tight and strumming by using the whole forearm will severely restrict the potential speed and fluency of your rhythm playing – so make sure that the strumming action comes from your wrist. It's a good idea to practise in front of a mirror, or record a video of yourself playing guitar, so that you can see if you're using the right technique.

Chord Technique

Be careful not to over-grip with the fretting-hand thumb on the back of the neck as this will cause muscle fatigue and tend to limit freedom of the thumb to move. The fretting-hand thumb must move freely when changing chords. If the thumb remains static this restricts the optimum positioning of the fingers for the next chord, which may result in unnecessary stretching and the involuntary dampening of certain strings (as the fingers are not positioned upright on their tips). Be aware that for the fingers to move freely the wrist, elbow and shoulder must be flexible and relaxed. Make sure your standing or sitting position doesn't restrict the movement of your hands and arms.

Make sure you hold the thumb in opposition to the fingers, behind the neck, but don't press too hard (see below).

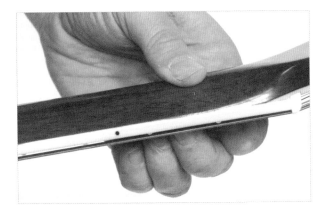

Basics

Folk

Blues

Rock 'n'Roll

Pop Rock

Heavy Rock

Alt. Rock

Other Styles

Skills

Rhythm

Chords

More

Simple Chord Sequences

Many songs consist of a short chord sequence that is repeated throughout. Once you have learnt a couple of basic chord shapes you can start playing a chord sequence by changing from one chord to another. It's then only a short step before you can play the chords to a complete song.

Minor Chords

Begin by strumming downwards four times on an E minor chord, then without stopping change to A minor and play another four strums, keeping the same tempo. Without stopping or hesitating, move your fingers back to E minor and continue strumming so that the whole sequence begins again.

Notice the similarity of the E minor and A minor chord shapes: the second and third fingers are used at the second fret in both chords, the only difference being that they move from the A and D strings in E minor to the adjacent D and G strings in A minor. Try to keep this in mind when you change between these chords, so that you can minimize the amount of finger movement you make – this will make changing between the chords easier and quicker.

Major Chords

Begin by playing four downstrums on a G major chord then, without stopping, move your fingers to D major and play another four strums. Repeat the sequence from the beginning by changing back to G major. Try to keep an even tempo throughout

Basics

Folk

Blues

Rock
'n'Roll

Pop
Rock

Heavy
Rock

Alt.
Rock

Other
Styles

Skills

Rhythm

Chords

More

and practise slowly until you are able to change between the chords without pausing or hesitating. Notice how the third finger stays at the third fret for both G and D major. Use this as a pivot point to lead the chord change. Try to move all three fretting fingers as one shape when changing chord, rather than placing the fingers on one at a time; this will make the chord changes smoother.

Combining Chords

Once you feel fully familiar with the four chord shapes, try and combine them in this four-chord sequence, playing four downstrums for each chord.

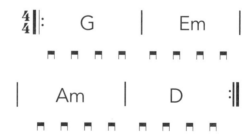

Basics

Folk

Blues

Rock 'n'Roll

Pop Rock

Heavy Rock

Alt. Rock

Other Styles

Skills

Rhythm

Chords

More

1. Look for any links between the different chord fingerings so that you can minimize the amount of finger movement you need to make.

2. Remember to place the fingers for each complete chord shape on the fretboard together, rather than finger by finger.

3. Practise very slowly so that you don't develop a habit of slowing down or stopping between chord changes.

Basics

Folk

Blues

Rock 'n'Roll

Pop Rock

Heavy Rock

Alt. Rock

Other Styles

Skills

Rhythm

Chords

More

G
Major

Chord Spelling
1st (G), 3rd (B), 5th (D)

Em
Minor

Chord Spelling
1st (E), ♭3rd (G), 5th (B)

Am
Minor

Chord Spelling
1st (A), ♭3rd (C), 5th (E)

D
Major

Chord Spelling
1st (D), 3rd (F♯), 5th (A)

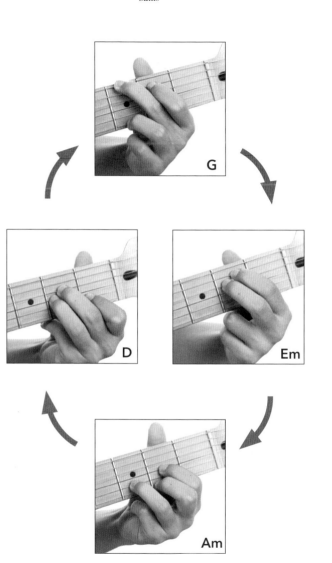

Basics

Folk

Blues

Rock 'n'Roll

Pop Rock

Heavy Rock

Alt. Rock

Other Styles

Skills

Rhythm

Chords

More

Basics

Folk

Blues

Rock
'n'Roll

Pop
Rock

Heavy
Rock

Alt.
Rock

Other
Styles

Skills

Rhythm

Chords

More

Putting Chords Together

When playing chords it's important to learn
how to change fluently between them without
leaving gaps. This can be a difficult skill to
master, but luckily there are a few shortcuts
you can take.

Minimum Movement Principle

It's essential that chord changes are crisp,
prompt, and in time. This can be made easier
if following the 'minimum movement principle',
which involves making only the smallest finger
movement necessary between chords, and
avoiding taking fingers off notes or frets only to
put them back on again for the next chord.

Excess movement between chords is what slows
chord changes down; the less your fingers move, the
faster your chord changes will be.

Shared Notes

Always look for links, or common notes, between consecutive chords, so you can minimize the amount of finger movement needed when changing chords. You may be able to keep some fingers on, or at least slide them (on the guitar) along a string to the next chord.

Basics

Folk

Blues

Rock 'n'Roll

Pop Rock

Heavy Rock

Alt. Rock

Other Styles

Skills

Rhythm

Chords

More

Basics

Folk

Blues

Rock
'n'Roll

Pop
Rock

Heavy
Rock

Alt.
Rock

Other
Styles

Skills

Rhythm

Chords

More

Smooth Chord Changes

Opposite you'll see a chord progression in A minor for the guitar. Between each new chord there's a return to the basic A minor chord.

Notice the common notes between the chords shown: the first finger stays on the first fret and the second finger stays on the second fret throughout.

- The open position A minor and F major chords both include the note C (first fret on the B string).

- The C major chord also includes this note, and, in addition, has another note in common with the A minor chord (E on the second fret of the D string). Between Am and C only the third finger needs to be moved.

- Notice, too, how E major is the same 'shape' as Am – just on different strings.

Basics

Folk

Blues

Rock
'n'Roll

Pop
Rock

Heavy
Rock

Alt.
Rock

Other
Styles

Skills

Rhythm

Chords

More

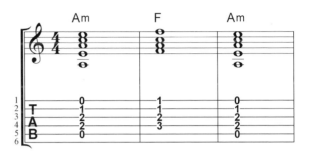

Basics

Folk

Blues

Rock
'n'Roll

Pop
Rock

Heavy
Rock

Alt.
Rock

Other
Styles

Skills

Rhythm

Chords

More

Following the principle of minimum movement saves time and makes the chord changes smoother. No matter how remote a chord change appears to be, there will always be some kind of link between the chords; once spotted, this will make changing between them easier.

'Open Vamp' Strum

If all else fails, there is a 'pro-trick' you can use that will mask any gap between chord changes: using an 'open vamp' strum. This simply involves strumming the open strings while your fingers move between chords. While not ideal, it does mean that the overall fluency and momentum of the performance is maintained. In fact, some players actually make a feature of this technique to bring out accents within their rhythm playing. Whatever technique you use, the golden rule in rhythm playing when you come across difficult passages is 'never stop – always keep strumming'.

Basics

Folk

Blues

Rock
'n'Roll

Pop
Rock

Heavy
Rock

Alt.
Rock

Other
Styles

Skills

Rhythm

Chords

More

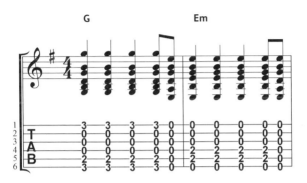

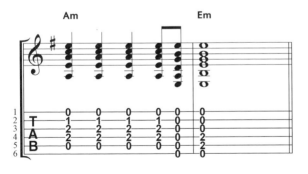

Basics

Folk

Blues

Rock 'n'Roll

Pop Rock

Heavy Rock

Alt. Rock

Other Styles

Skills

Rhythm

Chords

More

Power Chords

Playing only selected notes from a chord can actually give a stronger sound than playing the whole chord: you can get a tighter and more easily controlled sound by just using two or three notes from a chord.

Fifths

In rock music, instead of full chords, abbreviated versions just using the root and fifth note are often played. These 'fifth chords' are commonly called 'power chords'. Apart from the tone, one of the main advantages of using fifths is that it's much easier to move quickly from chord to chord because there are only a couple of fingers involved. To play a fifth power chord, simply fret a note on any bass string and add a note two frets up on the adjacent higher string. Opposite you'll see a typical 1970s rock riff, Octave notes could be used as well as the fifth to give a heavier sound.

Basics

Folk

Blues

Rock 'n'Roll

Pop Rock

Heavy Rock

Alt. Rock

Other Styles

Skills

Rhythm

Chords

More

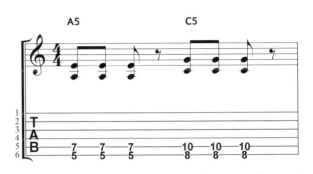

Basics

Folk

Blues

Rock
'n'Roll

Pop
Rock

Heavy
Rock

Alt.
Rock

Other
Styles

Skills

Rhythm

Chords

More

Slides

Sliding from one note or chord to another is a great way of creating a seamless legato sound that can make your playing sound relaxed and effortless. The technique also provides an easy way of adding passing notes to make your playing unique and inventive.

ABOVE: The slide technique: a slide from a high note to a low note using heavy sustain.

Basics

Folk

Blues

Rock
'n'Roll

Pop
Rock

Heavy
Rock

Alt.
Rock

Other
Styles

Skills

Rhythm

Chords

More

Slide Technique

To slide a note means to fret it and then, while maintaining the fretting pressure, to move the finger to another fret on the same string without picking the note again. The second note is sounded only because of the continued pressure of the fretting hand.

In a standard slide you only hear the first and last notes. However, you can also play a 'glissando' type of slide, in which all the intervening notes are also sounded.

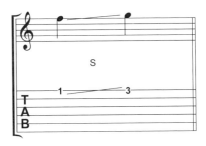

ABOVE: Slide: pick the F note then, using the force of the fretting finger alone, sound the G note by quickly sliding the first finger along the E string.

Basics

Folk

Blues

Rock
'n'Roll

Pop
Rock

Heavy
Rock

Alt.
Rock

Other
Styles

Skills

Rhythm

Chords

More

Controlling the amount of grip with the fretting hand is the secret to good sliding. You should try to ensure that the thumb at the back of the guitar neck relaxes its grip when you are in the process of sliding a note up or down. This doesn't mean that the thumb needs to be released totally, but simply that it shouldn't be squeezing tightly against the back of the guitar neck. However, just as your hand reaches the note that you want to slide into, the thumb should squeeze the neck slightly harder to act as a brake, preventing your fingers sliding beyond the destination fret.

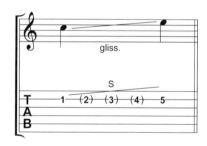

ABOVE: Glissando slide: pick the C note then, using the force of the fretting finger, slide along the B string up to the E note, allowing the notes in between to sound.

Sliding Chords

The guitar is one of the few instruments on which you can slide chords up and down, changing their pitch easily and smoothly; the technique creates a fluidity and smoothness of sound that piano players can only dream of! Because slides are so natural to the guitar they form a core component of any good rhythm-guitarist's technique. Slides are used by guitarists in nearly all musical styles, from metal and blues to country and ska.

When sliding chords it's important to ensure that the chord shape is maintained, so that one finger doesn't end up a fret ahead of the rest! The trick is to achieve a neutral balance whereby the chord shape is kept under control, yet at the same time the fingers are relaxed enough to slide up or down the fingerboard.

Playing fifth 'power chords', where only two notes are fretted, is the ideal introduction to sliding chords.

Basics

Folk

Blues

Rock
'n'Roll

Pop
Rock

Heavy
Rock

Alt.
Rock

Other
Styles

Skills

Rhythm

Chords

More

Basics

Folk

Blues

Rock
'n'Roll

Pop
Rock

Heavy
Rock

Alt.
Rock

Other
Styles

Skills

Rhythm

Chords

More

Playing power chords with a copious amount of distortion is the easiest way to begin chord sliding; the distortion will provide sustain, which will encourage you not to grip too hard when sliding the chords. Using ascending slides (raising the pitch of a chord) is easier at first – the volume tends to disappear quite quickly with descending slides.

Basics

Folk

Blues

Rock 'n'Roll

Pop Rock

Heavy Rock

Alt. Rock

Other Styles

Skills

Rhythm

Chords

More

Fingerpicking

Fingerpicking can provide a really interesting
alternative to strumming. The technique is not
just confined to classical or folk guitarists – many
rock and pop players also use fingerpicking as a
method of bringing melodic interest to a chord
progression and as a way of introducing musical
subtleties to a song.

Basics

Folk

Blues

Rock
'n'Roll

Pop
Rock

Heavy
Rock

Alt.
Rock

Other
Styles

Skills

Rhythm

Chords

More

Fingering

In music notation for fingerpicking, each picking finger is identified by a letter:

p = thumb

i   = index finger

m = middle finger

a = ring finger

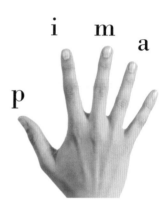

As it is much shorter than the others, the little finger is rarely used in fingerpicking.

Tip: It's easier to fingerpick if you let your fingernails grow a little. Using nails to pick the strings will also give you a crisper, clearer and stronger sound.

The thumb is mostly used for playing the bass strings (the lowest three strings), while the fingers are used for playing the treble strings. There are many different ways of fingerpicking, but one of the easiest is to use the 'a' finger for picking the first string, the 'm' finger for the second string and the 'i' finger for the third string.

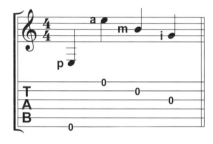

Picking Patterns

Basics

Folk

Blues

Rock
'n'Roll

Pop
Rock

Heavy
Rock

Alt.
Rock

Other
Styles

Skills

Rhythm

Chords

More

Many guitarists use a repetitive fingerpicking pattern throughout a song to create a continuity of sound. Picking patterns nearly always begin by playing the root note of the chord (i.e. the note that gives the letter name to the chord) on the

Basics

Folk

Blues

Rock
'n'Roll

Pop
Rock

Heavy
Rock

Alt.
Rock

Other
Styles

Skills

Rhythm

Chords

More

bass string using the thumb. For example, the low
E string would be the first note of a pattern when
fingerpicking on a chord of E minor, and the open
A string would be the first note when fingerpicking
on a chord of A minor.

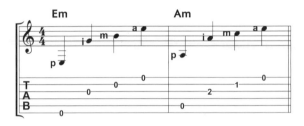

If the picking pattern on a chord is repeated then
sometimes a different bass is used the second time.
This will normally be another note from the chord,
usually the adjacent bass string. This technique can
completely transform a simple chord progression,
making it sound quite complex because of the
moving bass line. This style of fingerpicking is
known as 'alternating bass'.

In some musical styles, more complex picking patterns might be used on the treble strings. It is best to practise these types of patterns on one chord until the picking pattern feels totally comfortable. Once you are familiar with a pattern it's relatively easy to apply it to a chord progression. You just need to take care about which bass note to pick on each chord, ensuring you use the root note as your starting point.

Fingerpicking Em (right hand)

Basics

Folk

Blues

Rock
'n'Roll

Pop
Rock

Heavy
Rock

Alt.
Rock

Other
Styles

Skills

Rhythm

Chords

More

Plectrum Technique

Most electric guitarists want to play fast, and developing great speed starts with having proper control over your plectrum. If you start by holding the plectrum the wrong way you can develop habits that will make it hard to become a fast and accurate player.

Gripping the Plectrum

The best method is to grip the plectrum between the thumb and index finger. Position the plectrum so that its point is about half a centimetre (¼ of an inch) beyond the fingertip. Use only the tip of the plectrum to pick the strings or you will create a physical resistance that will slow down your playing. However, bear in mind that if you show too little plectrum you might end up missing the string altogether. Experiment until you get just the right balance. Also, be mindful of how you grip the plectrum. If you use too much pressure your hand muscles will tighten and so reduce your fluency, but if you hold it too loosely you'll keep dropping it.

Hold the plectrum so that it's in line with your fingernail. Avoid holding it at right angles to your index finger, as this will cause your wrist to lock.

Basics

Folk

Blues

Rock
'n'Roll

Pop
Rock

Heavy
Rock

Alt.
Rock

Other
Styles

Skills

Rhythm

Chords

More

ABOVE: How to hold your plectrum. Notice the angle and amount of plectrum tip showing.

Basics

Folk

Blues

Rock
'n'Roll

Pop
Rock

Heavy
Rock

Alt.
Rock

Other
Styles

Skills

Rhythm

Chords

More

Alternate Picking

If you want to achieve any degree of speed with
the plectrum for lead playing then it's best to use
'alternate picking' as the mainstay of your plectrum
technique. This involves alternating downstrokes
and upstrokes. Alternate picking is the most logical
and economical way of playing, since once you have
picked a string downwards, the plectrum will then
be ideally positioned to pick upwards, whereas if you
try to play two downstrokes in a row you will need
to raise the plectrum back up before you can strike
the string again.

Downstroke   Upstroke

When alternating down- and upstrokes, make sure that the picking action is generated by swivelling the wrist; try to avoid moving the elbow up and down as this will make your picking style much too cumbersome and will hamper your fluency. For fast lead playing, alternate picking and a relaxed wrist action are the fundamental requirements.

Picking Exercises

Alternate picking can be done on any string. To start, you can begin by practising alternate picking on the open sixth string. Once you have a secure plectrum technique you can make your licks sound faster by doubling, or even quadrupling, your picking on some notes. The fretting hand may be moving quite slowly, but the lick will sound more mobile because of the activity of the picking hand.

Practise this technique at first by playing scales with double and quadruple picking.

Basics

Folk

Blues

Rock 'n'Roll

Pop Rock

Heavy Rock

Alt. Rock

Other Styles

Skills

Rhythm

Chords

More

Basics

Folk

Blues

Rock
'n'Roll

Pop
Rock

Heavy
Rock

Alt.
Rock

Other
Styles

Skills

Rhythm

Chords

More

A fast rock sound can be achieved by mixing fretted notes with an open string – while the right hand keeps picking with alternate down- and upstrokes.

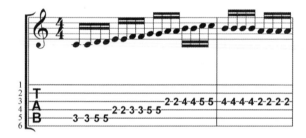

ABOVE: C major scale, played ascending with double picking and descending with quadruple picking.

Triplet Picking

A great way of making your playing sound super-fast is to use triplet picking patterns. Because these patterns cut across the standard $\frac{4}{4}$ rhythm, they give the impression of being much faster than they really are. This repeated 'down-up-down' picking style can give a rolling or galloping effect.

The term 'triplet' here refers only to the three-part picking action; the rhythm doesn't have to be a triplet in the traditional musical sense.

Basics

Folk

Blues

Rock 'n'Roll

Pop Rock

Heavy Rock

Alt. Rock

Other Styles

Skills

Rhythm

Chords

More

String Damping

Nearly all rock and blues players use string damping as a way of controlling the guitar's volume and tone. By resting the side of the strumming hand lightly on the strings, close to the saddle, a choked or muted sound can be achieved by deadening the sustain of the strings.

ABOVE: String damping, using 'palm muting' technique: the edge of the fretting hand rests against the strings next to the bridge; the hand stays in position when you strum, to mute the strings.

Basics

Folk

Blues

Rock 'n'Roll

Pop Rock

Heavy Rock

Alt. Rock

Other Styles

Skills

Rhythm

Chords

More

Damping Technique

String damping is an essential technique for varying the tone and volume of your guitar playing. The technique can be used after a note or chord has been played to achieve a short and detached 'staccato' effect. Damping can also be used to bring out accents in a rhythm, by maintaining the muting effect throughout and releasing only intermittently on the beats to be accented.

Strumming-hand Damping

To learn this technique, first strum slowly across all the open strings to hear the natural sound of the guitar. Then, place your strumming hand at a 90-degree angle to the strings, close to the saddle, with the side of the hand (in line with the little finger) pressing lightly against all six strings. Maintain contact with the strings with the edge of your hand, and then rotate the hand towards the strings and

Basics

Folk

Blues

Rock 'n'Roll

Pop Rock

Heavy Rock

Alt. Rock

Other Styles

Skills

Rhythm

Chords

More

235

Basics

Folk

Blues

Rock
'n'Roll

Pop
Rock

Heavy
Rock

Alt.
Rock

Other
Styles

Skills

Rhythm

Chords

More

strum again. The pressure of the hand against the strings will dampen the volume and sustain – this is known as 'palm muting'. Notice how this is very different from the normal sound of strummed open strings. Now try this again with an E minor chord.

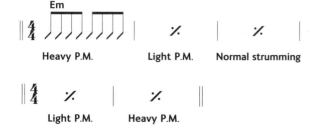

ABOVE: Palm muting. Measure 1: press firmly against the strings. M. 2: lighten the pressure. M. 3: release damping hand. M. 4: re-apply damping hand, increasing pressure in the final measure.

When you use string damping it's not necessary to always strum all the strings of the chord; often – particularly in rock styles – it's better just to strum the bass string and a couple of others. Vary the

Basics

Folk

Blues

Rock
'n'Roll

Pop
Rock

Heavy
Rock

Alt.
Rock

Other
Styles

Skills

Rhythm

Chords

More

amount of pressure with which the side of the hand rests on the strings: if you press too hard the notes will just become dead thuds, but if you press too lightly the strings will start to ring and sustain again. Be aware that it's all too easy at first to pull the damping hand away from the strings as you begin to strum, so losing the muting effect. Although it may take a while to gain control of this technique, and to strike the right balance of pressure and release, it's well worth the effort as string damping is an essential tool that will broaden your technique.

ABOVE: Palm muting can also be used in lead playing, resulting in a very staccato sound (with all the notes short and detached). This technique is often used in funk music.

Basics

Folk

Blues

Rock
'n'Roll

Pop
Rock

Heavy
Rock

Alt.
Rock

Other
Styles

Skills

Rhythm

Chords

More

Alternative Tunings

Discover a new range of beautiful chordal harmonies by simply tuning your guitar in a different way. If you sometimes start to feel restricted by sticking to the same chord shapes you've played before, then experimenting with alternative tunings is a great way of generating some fresh sounds and ideas.

Dropped D Tuning

There are numerous ways in which a guitar can be retuned, but the simplest and most commonly used is 'dropped D tuning'. All you need to do is lower the pitch of the low E string by a whole step until it reaches the note of D (an octave lower than the open fourth string). You can check that you've retuned correctly by playing on the seventh fret of the sixth string and comparing the note to the open fifth string they should produce exactly the same pitch.

Basics

Folk

Blues

Rock 'n'Roll

Pop Rock

Heavy Rock

Alt. Rock

Other Styles

Skills

Rhythm

Chords

More

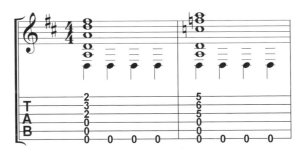

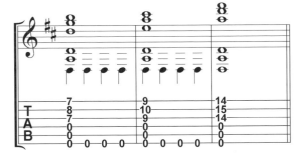

Dropped D tuning is perfect for playing songs in the keys of D major or D minor. Having the low D bass string is almost like having your own built-in bass player – it can add great solidity and power to your sound. To make the most of this

Basics

Folk

Blues

Rock
'n'Roll

Pop
Rock

Heavy
Rock

Alt.
Rock

Other
Styles

Skills

Rhythm

Chords

More

bass effect many guitarists use the low D string as a 'drone' – i.e. they repeatedly play this low D note while moving chord shapes up and down the fingerboard. Moving a simple D major shape up the fingerboard while playing a low D drone produces a very effective sound.

D Modal Tuning

Tuning the sixth, second and first strings down a whole step creates what is known as 'D modal tuning': D A D G A D. When you need to reach this tuning unaided just remember that the A, D and G strings are tuned as normal. Playing the open D string will give you the pitch for the

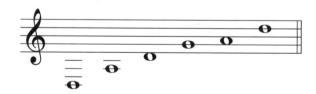

lowered sixth string when it is played at the 12th fret. Playing the A string at the 12th fret will give you the pitch to tune the second string down to, and playing the D string at the 12th fret will give you the pitch to tune the first string down to. Once the guitar is correctly tuned it will give you a Dsus4 chord when the open strings are all strummed, thus creating instant ambiguity and a sense of interest.

When first using this tuning, playing in the key of D will prove the easiest: by placing the first finger on the second fret of the G string you will make a nice deep-sounding D major (D5) chord.

Traditional chord shapes will not work in the same way with any altered tuning, so it's really a case of experimenting to find chord sounds that you like. The secret is to be adventurous and see what ideas you can come up with when freed from the restrictions of conventional chord shapes.

Basics

Folk

Blues

Rock
'n'Roll

Pop
Rock

Heavy
Rock

Alt.
Rock

Other
Styles

Skills

Rhythm

Chords

More

Basics

Folk

Blues

Rock
'n'Roll

Pop
Rock

Heavy
Rock

Alt.
Rock

Other
Styles

Skills

Rhythm

Chords

More

10

Rhythm

A good understanding of rhythm is crucial
when playing strumming patterns. This
chapter takes you back to the basics, looking
at specific note and rest values, simple rhythm
notation, and time signatures. Also includes
tips on general timing and keeping a
steady pulse.

Basics

Folk

Blues

Rock
'n'Roll

Pop
Rock

Heavy
Rock

Alt.
Rock

Other
Styles

Skills

Rhythm

Chords

More

Basics

Folk

Blues

Rock
'n'Roll

Pop
Rock

Heavy
Rock

Alt.
Rock

Other
Styles

Skills

Rhythm

Chords

More

Rhythm

Rhythm is the essential ingredient of all music. It is important in all styles of music, although it is more obvious in some types of music, such as African drumming, than others, such as plainsong.

Rhythm includes all aspects of music to do with time. These can fall into the following categories:

Tempo

This is the speed of the music, which can be from very slow to very fast. It can also speed up or slow down.

Metre

The metre of a piece of music is the number of beats in each bar and how they are grouped. Most rock and pop music, for instance, is in 4/4 (four beats to a bar), whereas waltzes are in 3/4 (three beats a bar).

Rhythm

This is the actual sequence of note-values that make up the music: three short notes followed by one long one and then two short ones, for instance. Most of this section will concentrate on how to read note values.

Basics

Folk

Blues

Rock 'n'Roll

Pop Rock

Heavy Rock

Alt. Rock

Other Styles

Skills

Rhythm

Chords

More

Basics

Folk

Blues

Rock 'n'Roll

Pop Rock

Heavy Rock

Alt. Rock

Other Styles

Skills

Rhythm

Chords

More

Keeping a Steady Pulse

The key to reading rhythm successfully is to be able to do it in time. To do this, you need to have a steady pulse beating in your head as you read and play the notes.

As practice, get hold of a clock or watch that makes a ticking noise every second. Clap your hands every time the clock ticks and keep going until you are exactly in time with the clock, clapping every second. You are clapping at 60 beats per minute (60b.p.m.)

Now clap twice for every tick of the clock, trying to make your claps as evenly-spaced as possible. You should be clapping twice a second, 120 times a minute, or 120 b.p.m.

Now clap four times for each tick of the clock, again aiming to make your claps as even and regular as possible. This speed is 240 b.p.m.

Basics

Folk

Blues

Rock
'n'Roll

Pop
Rock

Heavy
Rock

Alt.
Rock

Other
Styles

Skills

Rhythm

Chords

More

If possible when practising, get hold of a metronome, a device which gives out a steady pulse for whichever tempo you select. More on timing follows on the next few pages.

Basics

Folk

Blues

Rock
'n'Roll

Pop
Rock

Heavy
Rock

Alt.
Rock

Other
Styles

Skills

Rhythm

Chords

More

Timing

The most important skill any rhythm-guitar
player needs is the ability to maintain an
even tempo and keep in time with other band
members. It's essential that your rhythm playing
sits in the same groove as the other members of
the rhythm section.

Developing Timing Skills

Some people have a natural sense of rhythm and
timing that just needs nurturing, while others have
to concentrate on developing a secure sense of
timing. A simple test to evaluate your sense of
timing is to try and clap along to a recording by
one of your favourite bands. While listening to the
recording, focus your attention on the drums and
try to clap a regular beat that matches the main
rhythmic pulses within the song. Listen carefully
to your clapping and see if you can stay in time

Basics

Folk

Blues

Rock
'n'Roll

Pop
Rock

Heavy
Rock

Alt.
Rock

Other
Styles

Skills

Rhythm

Chords

More

throughout the whole song – stamina is an important aspect of rhythm playing. Before you try to play through a song make sure that you have mastered any technical challenges, such as awkward chord changes, in advance. Otherwise, the temptation will be to slow down when approaching the difficult

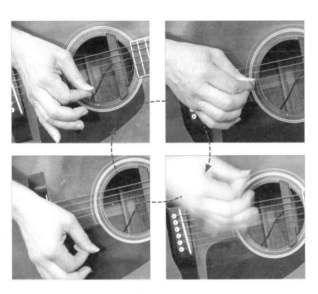

ABOVE: Keeping strict time is critical, even when varying the technique. Here, two quick alternating strums are followed by a full upstroke across all strings, then a solid downstroke.

Basics

Folk

Blues

Rock
'n'Roll

Pop
Rock

Heavy
Rock

Alt.
Rock

Other
Styles

Skills

Rhythm

Chords

More

bits and perhaps speed up on the easy bits. You
should try to avoid developing poor timing habits
from the start by always choosing a slow practice
tempo at which you can master the whole song
– difficult bits and all! Once you can play the
song without any mistakes or hesitations, it's
relatively easy to gradually increase the tempo
each time you practise.

Timing Aids

Ideally you should always try to practise your
rhythm playing with a device that keeps regular
time. The simplest method is to practise with
a metronome. This is a small mechanical or electronic
device that sounds a click on each beat. You can set
it to click in increments from a very slow to a super-
fast tempo. It's always best to practise anything new
at a slow tempo, increasing the metronome setting
by a couple of notches each time you've successfully
played it the whole way through.

A drum machine can be used instead of a
metronome. The advantage of the drum machine is
that you can set it to play back interesting drum
patterns to help inspire your strumming style. You
can programme the machine, or use preset patterns,
so that it emulates different musical genres.

Playing along to records is also a good method
of developing a secure sense of timing: the band
on the recording won't wait around if you lose
time or hesitate over a chord change. Because
there will be a longer space between beats, playing
along with songs at a slow tempo emphasizes any
timing inconsistencies – so don't forget to practise
a few ballads alongside the thrash metal!

Basics

Folk

Blues

Rock
'n'Roll

Pop
Rock

Heavy
Rock

Alt.
Rock

Other
Styles

Skills

Rhythm

Chords

More

Basics

Folk

Blues

Rock
'n'Roll

Pop
Rock

Heavy
Rock

Alt.
Rock

Other
Styles

Skills

Rhythm

Chords

More

Note Values

Notes are the main building blocks of every musical piece.

The position of the note on a particular stave tells you which note to play.

The look of the note tells you how long to sound the note and therefore gives you clues about the pulse of the music and how it relates to the time signature (see pages 290–309).

Notes can be grouped together and must be replaced by an equivalent rest (see pages 274–287) if no sound is to be played.

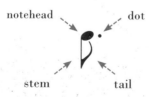

notehead · · dot

stem · · tail

beam

The below table provides a reminder of the relationship between notes of different lengths: these are looked at in more detail in the following pages.

Basics

Folk

Blues

Rock 'n'Roll

Pop Rock

Heavy Rock

Alt. Rock

Other Styles

Skills

Rhythm

Chords

More

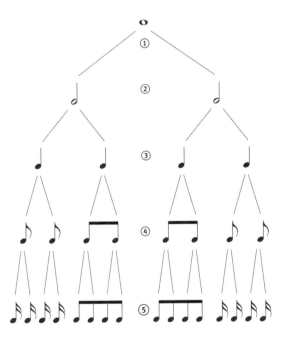

Whole note	①	Semibreve
Half notes	②	Minims
Quarter notes	③	Crotchets
Eighth notes	④	Quavers
Sixteenth notes	⑤	Semiquavers

Whole Note/Semibreve

A standard musical bar lasts for a whole note, or four quarter notes, so we will start with the whole note, or semibreve.

The semibreve is the longest note value covered in this section. It consists of just a hollow notehead, with no stem, flag, beams or dots.

A semibreve is equal to two minims, four crotchets or eight quavers.

Basics

Folk

Blues

Rock 'n'Roll

Pop Rock

Heavy Rock

Alt. Rock

Other Styles

Skills

Rhythm

Chords

More

1 2 3 4 5 6 7 8 1 2 3 4 5 6 7 8

1 2 3 4 1 2 3 4

1 2 3 4

Basics

Folk

Blues

Rock
'n'Roll

Pop
Rock

Heavy
Rock

Alt.
Rock

Other
Styles

Skills

Rhythm

Chords

More

Half Note/Minim

A minim is a note that fills half of a standard whole bar, hence the alternative name: half note.

A minim has a hollow notehead and a stem, but no tail or beam. The stem can go either up or down, depending on where the note is positioned on the stave.

A minim is equal to two crotchets, four quavers or eight semiquavers.

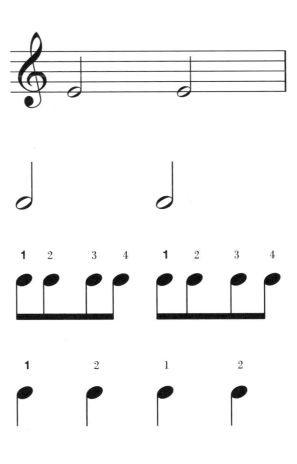

Basics

Folk

Blues

Rock 'n'Roll

Pop Rock

Heavy Rock

Alt. Rock

Other Styles

Skills

Rhythm

Chords

More

Basics

Folk

Blues

Rock
'n'Roll

Pop
Rock

Heavy
Rock

Alt.
Rock

Other
Styles

Skills

Rhythm

Chords

More

Quarter Note/Crotchet

A crotchet is a note that makes up a quarter of standard whole bar, hence the alternative name: quarter note.

A crotchet has a filled-in notehead and a stem, but no tail or beam. A crotchet's stem can go either up or down, depending on where the note is positioned on the stave.

A crotchet is equal to half a minim, two quavers or four semiquavers.

Rhythm

Basics

Folk

Blues

Rock
'n'Roll

Pop
Rock

Heavy
Rock

Alt.
Rock

Other
Styles

Skills

Rhythm

Chords

More

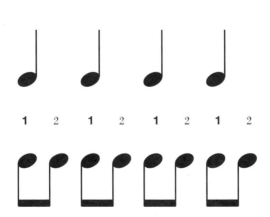

1   2   1   2   1   2   1   2

Basics

Folk

Blues

Rock
'n'Roll

Pop
Rock

Heavy
Rock

Alt.
Rock

Other
Styles

Skills

Rhythm

Chords

More

Eighth Note/Quaver

A quaver is a note that makes up an eighth of a standard whole bar, hence the alternative name: eighth note.

A quaver has a filled-in notehead, a stem, a tail and beams. A single quaver is written with its tail, but quavers are more commonly found in groups with a beam across, to make them easier to read.

A quaver is equal to two semiquavers.

This is a quaver rest
(see page 282–283).

quavers in groups of 2, 3
and 4 beams

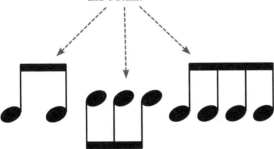

Basics

Folk

Blues

Rock
'n'Roll

Pop
Rock

Heavy
Rock

Alt.
Rock

Other
Styles

Skills

Rhythm

Chords

More

Basics

Folk

Blues

Rock
'n'Roll

Pop
Rock

Heavy
Rock

Alt.
Rock

Other
Styles

Skills

Rhythm

Chords

More

Sixteenth Note/Semiquaver

A semiquaver is a note that makes up a sixteenth of a standard whole bar, hence the alternative name: sixteenth note.

A semiquaver has a filled-in notehead, a stem and two tails, which become double beams when grouped with other semiquavers. They are usually found in groups, and can indicate a fast passage of music.

There are futher, shorter notes, with more tails. Demisemiquavers, for instance, last half as long as semiquavers.

Basics

Folk

Blues

Rock 'n'Roll

Pop Rock

Heavy Rock

Alt. Rock

Other Styles

Skills

Rhythm

Chords

More

semiquavers can be joined by beams to other

semiquavers or quavers

4 semiquavers
joined by a
double beam

2 semiquavers and

a quaver joined
by a double and
single beam
semiquaver,
quaver and

semiquaver joined
by a beam

There are two semiquavers to a quaver and

four semiquavers to a crotchet

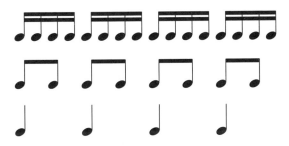

Dotted Notes

The length of the sound of a note can be increased by one half by adding a single dot to the right-hand side of the notehead.

These are known as 'dotted notes'. The table below shows the note length for dotted minims, dotted crotchets and dotted quavers relative to their undotted versions. These are looked at in more detail on the following pages.

Note	Length	Dotted Note	Length
♩	2	♩.	3
♩	1	♩.	$1\frac{1}{2}$
♪	$\frac{1}{2}$	♪.	$\frac{3}{4}$

Dotted Minim

A dotted minim has a hollow notehead, a stem and a dot but no flag or beam.

The stem can go either up or down, depending on where the note is positioned on the stave.

A dotted minim is worth six quavers or three crotchets.

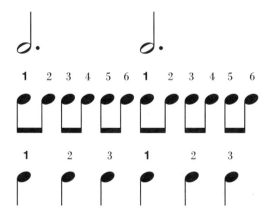

Basics · Folk · Blues · Rock 'n'Roll · Pop Rock · Heavy Rock · Alt. Rock · Other Styles · Skills · Rhythm · Chords · More

Basics

Folk

Blues

Rock 'n'Roll

Pop Rock

Heavy Rock

Alt. Rock

Other Styles

Skills

Rhythm

Chords

More

Dotted Crotchet

A dotted crotchet is a crotchet with a dot written after it.

Unlike the crotchet, which is worth two quavers, a dotted crotchet is worth three quavers.

The stem can go either up or down, depending on where the note is positioned on the stave.

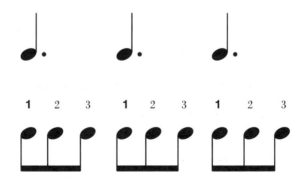

Dotted Quaver

Adding a dot to a quaver extends the quaver from two semiquavers to three semiquavers in length.

A dotted quaver stem may go either up or down, depending on its position on the stave. A dotted quaver may be joined to other notes with a beam.

Dotted Rhythm

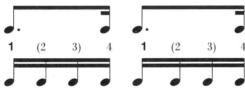

Scotch Snap Rhythm

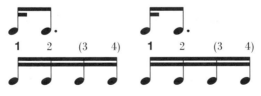

Basics

Folk

Blues

Rock
'n'Roll

Pop
Rock

Heavy
Rock

Alt.
Rock

Other
Styles

Skills

Rhythm

Chords

More

Basics

Folk

Blues

Rock
'n'Roll

Pop
Rock

Heavy
Rock

Alt.
Rock

Other
Styles

Skills

Rhythm

Chords

More

Triplets

Triplets are three identical notes tied together to fill the space of two equivalent notes.

They are indicated with a **3** above a group of three notes.

A note written as a triplet is always shorter than if the note was written normally. The three fit exactly and equally between them into the next note value up. For example, quaver triplets are shorter and quicker than ordinary quaver notes, and fit into the space of a crotchet.

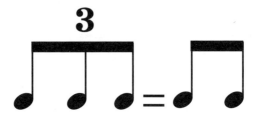

Basics

Folk

Blues

Rock
'n'Roll

Pop
Rock

Heavy
Rock

Alt.
Rock

Other
Styles

Skills

Rhythm

Chords

More

Notes to be played
as triplets are shown
with a bracket over or
under the notes and the
number three

Notes joined
by a beam
may just have
the number
and no bracket

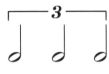

Three minim
triplets fit into the
time of a semibreve

Three crotchet
triplets fit into
the time of a
minim

Three quaver
triplets fit into
the time of a
crotchet

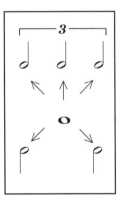

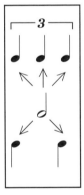

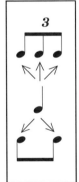

Three minim
triplets last the
same time as two
normal minims

Three crotchet
triplets last
the same time
as two normal
crotchets

Three quaver
triplets last
the same time
as two normal
quavers

Basics

Folk

Blues

Rock
'n'Roll

Pop
Rock

Heavy
Rock

Alt.
Rock

Other
Styles

Skills

Rhythm

Chords

More

Ties

Ties are curved lines that connect two notes of the same pitch. The line is drawn from notehead to notehead. The note is only played once, lasting the duration of both the tied notes added together.

Ties tend to be used in three situations:

- To create a note value for which there is no single symbol. For instance, this is useful for creating the length of a crotchet and a dotted quaver together.

- To extend a note across a barline.

- Where the note value is easier to read if it is written as more than one tied note.

Basics

Folk

Blues

Rock 'n'Roll

Pop Rock

Heavy Rock

Alt. Rock

Other Styles

Skills

Rhythm

Chords

More

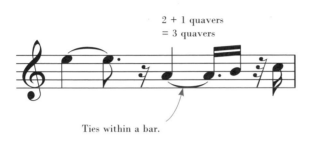

2 + 1 quavers
= 3 quavers

Ties within a bar.

Tie across a bar line.

Slurs

Slurs look like ties but they are not the same.

A slur indicates that the music within the start and end points should be played smoothly.

A slur connects notes of different pitches, and all of them are played.

A slur can stretch across several bars.

Basics

Folk

Blues

Rock 'n'Roll

Pop Rock

Heavy Rock

Alt. Rock

Other Styles

Skills

Rhythm

Chords

More

Basics

Folk

Blues

Rock
'n'Roll

Pop
Rock

Heavy
Rock

Alt.
Rock

Other
Styles

Skills

Rhythm

Chords

More

Rests

As well as notes, in music it is also essential to be able to indicate to the player the exact lengths of places where they should be silent. These spaces in the music are called 'rests'.

For each of the note values there is an equivalent rest.

Rests come in three types:

- Those that look like bricks (minim and semibreve)

- The crotchet rest, which is like a squiggle

- Those that look like keys (quaver and semiquaver)

These all occupy particular positions on the stave.

Basics

Folk

Blues

Rock
'n'Roll

Pop
Rock

Heavy
Rock

Alt.
Rock

Other
Styles

Skills

Rhythm

Chords

More

When looking at a bar of music it is important
to realize too that each bar must add up to the
number of beats set out at the beginning of the
piece. Where no notes are to be played, a rest is
put in their place to even out the beats.

For example, assuming a bar of four beats below,
the dotted minim only accounts for 3 of those
beats, so a crotchet rest (see pages 280–281) is
required.

The following pages will look at the most common
rests in more detail.

Basics

Folk

Blues

Rock
'n'Roll

Pop
Rock

Heavy
Rock

Alt.
Rock

Other
Styles

Skills

Rhythm

Chords

More

Whole Note/Semibreve Rest

The semibreve rest sits under the fourth line from the bottom line of the stave.

The semibreve rest has the same length as a semibreve note.

The standard musical bar contains four beats. A semibreve rest lasts for a whole bar of four beats.

If a bar only has three beats, the semibreve rest fills the whole bar too.

Note   Rest

Basics

Folk

Blues

Rock
'n'Roll

Pop
Rock

Heavy
Rock

Alt.
Rock

Other
Styles

Skills

Rhythm

Chords

More

Basics

Folk

Blues

Rock
'n'Roll

Pop
Rock

Heavy
Rock

Alt.
Rock

Other
Styles

Skills

Rhythm

Chords

More

Half Note/Minim Rest

The minim rest sits on top of the third line from the bottom line of the stave.

The minim rest has the same length as a half note, or minim.

The standard musical bar contains four beats.

A minim rest lasts for half a standard bar and so is equal to two beats.

Rhythm

Note   Rest

Basics

Folk

Blues

Rock 'n'Roll

Pop Rock

Heavy Rock

Alt. Rock

Other Styles

Skills

Rhythm

Chords

More

279

Basics

Folk

Blues

Rock
'n'Roll

Pop
Rock

Heavy
Rock

Alt.
Rock

Other
Styles

Skills

Rhythm

Chords

More

Quarter Note/Crotchet Rest

The crotchet rest is half the length of the minim rest.

It has the same length as a quarter note, or crotchet.

The standard musical bar contains four beats. A crotchet rest lasts for a quarter of a standard bar and so is equal to one beat.

Basics

Folk

Blues

Rock
'n'Roll

Pop
Rock

Heavy
Rock

Alt.
Rock

Other
Styles

Skills

Rhythm

Chords

More

Note   Rest

Basics

Folk

Blues

Rock
'n'Roll

Pop
Rock

Heavy
Rock

Alt.
Rock

Other
Styles

Skills

Rhythm

Chords

More

Eighth Note/Quaver Rest

The quaver rest is half the length of the crotchet rest. It has the same length as an eighth note, or quaver.

The standard musical bar contains four beats.

A quaver rest lasts for an eighth of a bar and so is equal to half a beat.

Basics

Folk

Blues

Rock
'n'Roll

Pop
Rock

Heavy
Rock

Alt.
Rock

Other
Styles

Skills

Rhythm

Chords

More

Note

Rest

Basics

Folk

Blues

Rock
'n'Roll

Pop
Rock

Heavy
Rock

Alt.
Rock

Other
Styles

Skills

Rhythm

Chords

More

Sixteenth Note/Semiquaver Rest

The semiquaver rest is half the length of the quaver rest. It has the same length as a sixteenth note, or semiquaver.

The standard musical bar contains four beats.

A semiquaver rest lasts for a sixteenth of a bar and so has a quarter of a beat.

Basics

Folk

Blues

Rock 'n'Roll

Pop Rock

Heavy Rock

Alt. Rock

Other Styles

Skills

Rhythm

Chords

More

Note   Rest

Dotted Note Rests

Rests may be dotted in the same way that notes are, with the dot extending the rest's value by half.

A dot placed after a crotchet rest, for example, will make that rest worth three quavers instead of two.

Opposite you will see the symbols for dotted notes along with their dotted rest equivalent.

Rhythm

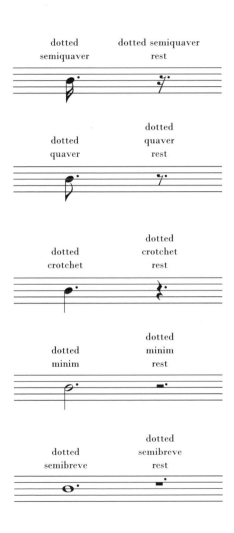

Basics

Folk

Blues

Rock 'n'Roll

Pop Rock

Heavy Rock

Alt. Rock

Other Styles

Skills

Rhythm

Chords

More

Basics

Folk

Blues

Rock
'n'Roll

Pop
Rock

Heavy
Rock

Alt.
Rock

Other
Styles

Skills

Rhythm

Chords

More

Rhythm Notation

Understanding how rhythms are written down will allow you to play through notated chord charts. The ability to notate your own rhythms is useful for passing the information to other players and as a memory aid. Even if you intend to rely mainly on tablature, a knowledge of rhythm notation will help you get the most out of the many song transcriptions that provide the full notation with the tab.

In rhythm notation, the notes are usually written without pitch. The note position on the stave doesn't change, and a diamond shape or line takes the place of the notehead.

The two tables opposite remind us of the notes and rests covered earlier, but show the notes in their rhythm notation form.

Rhythm

Name	Note	Rest	Duration in $\frac{4}{4}$ time
semibreve rest (whole rest)	◇	▬	4 beats
minim rest (half rest)	◇	▬	2 beats
crotchet rest (quarter rest)	♩	𝄽	1 beat
quaver rest (eighth rest)	♪	𝄾	½ a beat
semiquaver rest (16th rest)	♬	𝄿	¼ of a beat

Name	Note	Rest	Duration in $\frac{4}{4}$ time
Dotted minim (Dotted half note)	◇.	▬ .	3 beats
Dotted crotchet (Dotted quarter note)	♩.	𝄽 .	1½ beats
Dotted quaver (Dotted eighth note)	♪.	𝄾 .	¾ beat

Basics

Folk

Blues

Rock 'n'Roll

Pop Rock

Heavy Rock

Alt. Rock

Other Styles

Skills

Rhythm

Chords

More

Basics

Folk

Blues

Rock
'n'Roll

Pop
Rock

Heavy
Rock

Alt.
Rock

Other
Styles

Skills

Rhythm

Chords

More

Time Signatures

A time signature tells us how many notes and rests
will appear in each bar of music.

The time signature determines the pulse of the
music: whether it will feel fast or slow.

Time signatures create the framework around
which the notes can be written and understood.
They organize the sound to help the listener
understand what is happening inside the music.

In a lot of music, all the bars have the same
number of beats in them, specified by two numbers
written at the start of the music. This is called a
time signature.

A time signature consists of two numbers.

Basics

Folk

Blues

Rock 'n'Roll

Pop Rock

Heavy Rock

Alt. Rock

Other Styles

Skills

Rhythm

Chords

More

The top number tells you how many beats there are in each bar.

The bottom number tells you what sort of beat to use:

🌑 a 2 stands for half notes (minims)

🌑 a 4 stands for quarter notes (crotchets)

🌑 an 8 stands for eighth notes (quavers)

🌑 a 16 stands for sixteenth notes (semiquavers)

The following pages introduce some of the most common time signatures.

$$\frac{4}{4} \quad \frac{2}{2} \quad \frac{2}{4} \quad \frac{3}{4} \quad \frac{6}{8} \quad \frac{12}{8}$$

Basics

Folk

Blues

Rock
'n'Roll

Pop
Rock

Heavy
Rock

Alt.
Rock

Other
Styles

Skills

Rhythm

Chords

More

Four Quarter Notes Per Bar

The time signature shown with this symbol is four quarter notes/crotchets for each bar.

The top number shows that there are four beats in every bar.

The bottom number shows the length of each beat, in this case quarter notes/crotchets.

Basics

Folk

Blues

Rock 'n'Roll

Pop Rock

Heavy Rock

Alt. Rock

Other Styles

Skills

Rhythm

Chords

More

Basics

Folk

Blues

Rock
'n'Roll

Pop
Rock

Heavy
Rock

Alt.
Rock

Other
Styles

Skills

Rhythm

Chords

More

Common Time

This symbol is an alternative to the symbol on the previous page, and represents the same time signature.

The C (which is short for Common Time) means four quarter notes/crotchets for each bar.

There are four beats in every bar, with each of the four beats being quarter notes/crotchets.

Basics

Folk

Blues

Rock
'n'Roll

Pop
Rock

Heavy
Rock

Alt.
Rock

Other
Styles

Skills

Rhythm

Chords

More

Basics

Folk

Blues

Rock 'n'Roll

Pop Rock

Heavy Rock

Alt. Rock

Other Styles

Skills

Rhythm

Chords

More

Two Half Notes Per Bar

The time signature shown with this symbol represents two half notes/minims for each bar.

The top number shows that there are two beats in every bar.

The bottom number shows the length of each beat, in this case half notes/minims.

Basics

Folk

Blues

Rock 'n'Roll

Pop Rock

Heavy Rock

Alt. Rock

Other Styles

Skills

Rhythm

Chords

More

Basics

Folk

Blues

Rock
'n'Roll

Pop
Rock

Heavy
Rock

Alt.
Rock

Other
Styles

Skills

Rhythm

Chords

More

Cut Time

This symbol is an alternative to the symbol on the previous page, and represents the same time signature.

The $\math₵ $ (which is short for Cut Time) means two half notes/minims for each bar.

There are two beats in every bar, with each of the two beats being half notes/minims.

Basics

Folk

Blues

Rock
'n'Roll

Pop
Rock

Heavy
Rock

Alt.
Rock

Other
Styles

Skills

Rhythm

Chords

More

Basics

Folk

Blues

Rock
'n'Roll

Pop
Rock

Heavy
Rock

Alt.
Rock

Other
Styles

Skills

Rhythm

Chords

More

Two Quarter Notes Per Bar

The time signature shown with this symbol is two quarter notes/crotchets for each bar.

The top number shows that there are two beats in every bar.

The bottom number shows the length of each beat, in this case quarter notes/crotchets.

Basics

Folk

Blues

Rock
'n'Roll

Pop
Rock

Heavy
Rock

Alt.
Rock

Other
Styles

Skills

Rhythm

Chords

More

Basics

Folk

Blues

Rock
'n'Roll

Pop
Rock

Heavy
Rock

Alt.
Rock

Other
Styles

Skills

Rhythm

Chords

More

Three Quarter Notes Per Bar

The time signature shown with this symbol is three quarter notes/crotchets for each bar.

The top number shows that there are three beats in every bar.

The bottom number shows the length of each beat, in this case quarter notes/crotchets.

Basics

Folk

Blues

Rock 'n'Roll

Pop Rock

Heavy Rock

Alt. Rock

Other Styles

Skills

Rhythm

Chords

More

Basics

Folk

Blues

Rock
'n'Roll

Pop
Rock

Heavy
Rock

Alt.
Rock

Other
Styles

Skills

Rhythm

Chords

More

Six Eighth Notes Per Bar

The time signature shown with this symbol is six eighth notes/quavers for each bar.

The top number shows that there are six beats in every bar.

The bottom number shows the length of each beat, in this case, eighth notes/quavers.

In this time signature the six notes are grouped in threes.

Basics

Folk

Blues

Rock 'n'Roll

Pop Rock

Heavy Rock

Alt. Rock

Other Styles

Skills

Rhythm

Chords

More

Basics

Folk

Blues

Rock
'n'Roll

Pop
Rock

Heavy
Rock

Alt.
Rock

Other
Styles

Skills

Rhythm

Chords

More

Twelve Eighth Notes Per Bar

The time signature shown with this symbol is twelve eighth notes/quavers for each bar.

The top number shows that there are twelve beats in every bar.

The bottom number shows the length of each beat, in this case, eighth notes/quavers.

In this time signature the twelve notes are grouped in threes.

This time signature is commonly used in blues and jazz.

306

Basics

Folk

Blues

Rock 'n'Roll

Pop Rock

Heavy Rock

Alt. Rock

Other Styles

Skills

Rhythm

Chords

More

Basics

Folk

Blues

Rock
'n'Roll

Pop
Rock

Heavy
Rock

Alt.
Rock

Other
Styles

Skills

Rhythm

Chords

More

Time Signatures and Rhythm Notation

A bar in $\frac{2}{4}$ time.

A bar in $\frac{4}{4}$ time.

A bar in $\frac{3}{4}$ time.

A bar in $\frac{6}{8}$ time.

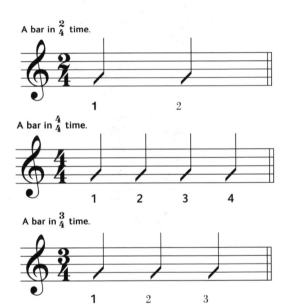

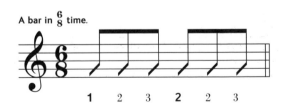

Basics

Folk

Blues

Rock 'n'Roll

Pop Rock

Heavy Rock

Alt. Rock

Other Styles

Skills

Rhythm

Chords

More

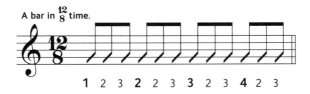

A bar in $\frac{12}{8}$ time.

1 2 3 **2** 2 3 **3** 2 3 **4** 2 3

Establishing the Time Signature

If you were just to play a long series of chords all of equal strength it would be hard for the listener to recognize any rhythmic structure in the music – in other words, they wouldn't be able to 'feel the groove'. So normally the first beat of each measure is slightly accented, as this helps the sense of rhythm in a piece of music. In 6/8 and 12/8 time, an accent is normally played on the first of each group of three notes. (If you're playing in a band it might be the drums or other instruments that emphasize these accents.)

Basics

Folk

Blues

Rock
'n'Roll

Pop
Rock

Heavy
Rock

Alt.
Rock

Other
Styles

Skills

Rhythm

Chords

More

Pulse

When you listen to a piece of music, there is
usually a clear, regular beat that you could tap
your foot to. Even when nothing happens on a
certain beat, you can usually still 'feel' a beat. If
you listen more closely, one beat usually sounds
more important than others, often giving a repeated
pattern like '1 2 3 4 1 2 3 4' or '1 2 3 1 2 3'.

Time signatures tell you what sort of beat pattern
the music has. In 2/4, 3/4 and 4/4, the pulse is the
crotchet. The strongest beat of each bar is always
the first, so in 2/4, there is a clear '1 2 1 2' pulse,
with '1' being stronger than '2'. In 3/4, there is a '1
2 3 1 2 3' pulse, with again 1 being stronger than
the other beats. In 4/4, the pulse is '1 2 3 4 1 2 3
4', with again 1 being strongest. In 2/2, there is a
minim pulse, the pattern being '1 2 1 2', with '1'
being the important beat.

Rhythm

In 4/4, 3/4 and 2/4, the main pulse is the crotchet

In these metres, each crotchet beat is slightly stressed, with the first beat of the bar stressed the most

In 2/2 and 3/2, the main pulse is the minim

In these metres, each minim beat is slightly stressed, with the first beat of the bar stressed the most

Basics

Folk

Blues

Rock 'n'Roll

Pop Rock

Heavy Rock

Alt. Rock

Other Styles

Skills

Rhythm

Chords

More

Basics

Folk

Blues

Rock
'n'Roll

Pop
Rock

Heavy
Rock

Alt.
Rock

Other
Styles

Skills

Rhythm

Chords

More

6/8, 9/8

Time signatures like 6/8 and 9/8 are slightly different from the metres looked at so far. There is a pulse of a dotted crotchet rather than a crotchet or minim, so there are three shorter notes to each beat rather than 2 or 4. This gives the music a skipping effect. The lazy, swung rhythms of jazz and blues are often in 6/8.

To count 6/8, you could either repeat '1 2 3 4 5 6 1 2 3 4 5 6', with a stress on '1' and '4' or repeat '1 2 1 2', fitting 3 quavers to each beat. The effect of a 6/8 metre can be achieved by repeating the phrase 'Hig-gle-dy Pig-gle-dy Hig-gle-dy Pig-gle-dy'.

9/8 also has a dotted crotchet pulse, with three dotted crotchets to a bar. It could be counted as '1 2 3 4 5 6 7 8 9 1 2 3 4 5 6 7 8 9' with stresses on '1', '4' and '7' or '1 2 3 1 2 3' with three quavers to each beat.

In 6/8, 9/8 and 12/8, the main pulse is the
dotted crotchet

In these metres, each dotted crotchet beat is slightly stressed,
with the first beat of the bar stressed the most

You can also count these metres in quavers,
stressing every third beat

Basics

Folk

Blues

Rock
'n'Roll

Pop
Rock

Heavy
Rock

Alt.
Rock

Other
Styles

Skills

Rhythm

Chords

More

Basics

Folk

Blues

Rock
'n'Roll

Pop
Rock

Heavy
Rock

Alt.
Rock

Other
Styles

Skills

Rhythm

Chords

More

Rhythm Charts

Standard chord charts are covered in the next
chapter, but often guitarists are required to know
about more detailed and complex charts known as
'rhythm charts'.

Chart Styles

Some rhythm charts can be quite elaborate and
may include a fully notated rhythm part, as well
as detailed instructions about dynamics and tempo.
Others may contain notated rhythms only at the
beginning, in order to establish the feel of the
song, with further rhythm notation only being
used where specific rhythmic accents or features
occur. The type of rhythm charts you come across
will depend on the context and the transcriber's
personal preferences.

Basics

Folk

Blues

Rock
'n'Roll

Pop
Rock

Heavy
Rock

Alt.
Rock

Other
Styles

Skills

Rhythm

Chords

More

Dynamic Markings

Symbols are often used in rhythm charts to indicate changes in volume – e.g. when you should play softly and when you should strum strongly. The symbols do not refer to any precise decibel volume level, instead their main function is to highlight changes in overall volume.

The most common dynamic markings are shown on the following page.

Articulation

Accents, where certain individual beats are played stronger than others, are marked by this sign: >. The letters 'sfz' (sforzando) may be also used to indicate an accent. See page 317 for a table of articulation markings.

Basics

Folk

Blues

Rock
'n'Roll

Pop
Rock

Heavy
Rock

Alt.
Rock

Other
Styles

Skills

Rhythm

Chords

More

Dynamics

Dynamics are markings telling the player how loudly to play. They are usually written under the note(s) to which they refer.

Symbol	Italian term	Meaning
pp	pianissimo	very quiet
p	piano	quiet
mp	mezzo piano	fairly quiet
mf	mezzoforte	fairly loud
f	forte	loud
ff	fortissimo	very loud
◁	crescendo (cresc.)	getting louder
▷	diminuendo (dim.)	getting quieter

Articulation

These marks are written above or below the notes and show how to play the notes.

.	*staccato*	short
>	*accento*	accented
∧	*marcato*	louder accent
—	*tenuto*	slightly stressed
⌒	*legato*	slur, smooth
sfz	*sforzando*	forced, heavy accent
fp	*fortepiano*	loud attack then quiet
⌒	*fermata*	hold, pause
√	*all' ottava*	one octave higher than written
8vb	*ottava bassa*	one octave lower than written
tr ⌇		trill

Basics

Folk

Blues

Rock 'n'Roll

Pop Rock

Heavy Rock

Alt. Rock

Other Styles

Skills

Rhythm

Chords

More

Basics

Folk

Blues

Rock
'n'Roll

Pop
Rock

Heavy
Rock

Alt.
Rock

Other
Styles

Skills

Rhythm

Chords

More

Tempo

Most rhythm charts will contain an indication of the speed at which the music should be played; this is usually written at the start of the music. The tempo indication may appear in either traditional Italian musical terms or their English equivalents. Alternatively, a metronome marking may be shown to indicate the exact number of beats per minute (b.p.m.).

The most common tempos are shown below.

Italian Term	Meaning	Approx speed
Largo	very slow	40–60 b.p.m.
Adagio	slow	50–75 b.p.m.
Andante	walking pace	75–100 b.p.m.
Moderato	moderate tempo	100–120 b.p.m.
Allegro	fast	120–160 b.p.m.
Presto	very quick	160–200 b.p.m.

318

Basics

Folk

Blues

Rock
'n'Roll

Pop
Rock

Heavy
Rock

Alt.
Rock

Other
Styles

Skills

Rhythm

Chords

More

Some music may contain changes in tempo.
These are usually indicated through the use of
Italian terms.

Italian Term	Meaning
Accel.	(an abbreviation of *accelerando*) means play gradually faster.
A tempo	indicates that you should resume the normal tempo after a deviation.
Meno mosso	(less movement) means that you should slow down at once.
Rall.	(an abbreviation of *rallentando*) means play gradually slower.
Rit.	(an abbreviation of *ritenuto*) means to hold back the tempo.
Ad lib.	(an abbreviation of *ad libitum*) means to perform freely – performer decides

Other Useful Symbols

D.C. al Fine	Return to the beginning and play to *Fine* (end).
D.S. al Fine	Return to 𝄋 and play to *Fine*.
D.C. al Coda	Return to the beginning, play to ⊕ and skip to Coda.
D.S. al Coda	Return to 𝄋 , play to ⊕ and skip to Coda.

:‖ Return to the beginning or nearest repeat sign. ‖:

Playing Rhythm Charts

Opposite you'll see a sample rhythm chart, incorporating some of the terms and symbols described in the previous pages. Refer to pages 252–273 if you need to be reminded of the note values.

Rhythm

Basics

Folk

Blues

Rock 'n'Roll

Pop Rock

Heavy Rock

Alt. Rock

Other Styles

Skills

Rhythm

Chords

More

Basics

Folk

Blues

Rock
'n'Roll

Pop
Rock

Heavy
Rock

Alt.
Rock

Other
Styles

Skills

Rhythm

Chords

More

Basic Strum Patterns

On the next few pages you'll find several examples of popular strumming patterns.

It's a good idea to start by playing all the progressions using just four downstrums per measure – this way you'll become familiar with the chord changes before tackling the strum patterns.

In nearly all styles of music, there is no need to strum all the strings on every beat – feel free to add variety, particularly by omitting some bass strings on upstrokes and some treble strings on downstrokes.

On pages 326–327 we'll look at some of the examples shown earlier in this book in more detail.

Basics

Folk

Blues

Rock 'n'Roll

Pop Rock

Heavy Rock

Alt. Rock

Other Styles

Skills

Rhythm

Chords

More

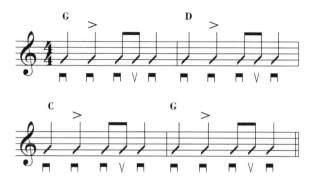

ABOVE: The second beat of the measure is accented to create dynamic variety. An upstroke is used after the third beat of the measure.

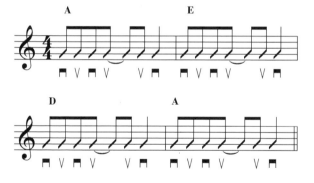

ABOVE: This pattern uses a mixture of down- and upstrokes, but notice how the fourth strum and the last strum are held longer than the others. This variety creates an effective rhythm.

Basics

Folk

Blues

Rock 'n'Roll

Pop Rock

Heavy Rock

Alt. Rock

Other Styles

Skills

Rhythm

Chords

More

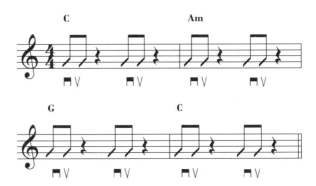

ABOVE: A simple down-up strum pattern, but the use of rests creates a very distinctive rhythmic effect.

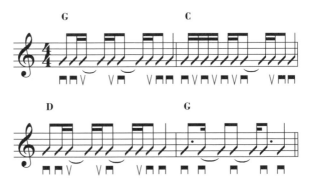

ABOVE: This 'Bo Diddley' type pattern is a good example of how to use rhythmic variations: notice that measures 1 and 3 are the same, while measures 2 and 4 are each variations on the first measure.

Basics

Folk

Blues

Rock
'n'Roll

Pop
Rock

Heavy
Rock

Alt.
Rock

Other
Styles

Skills

Rhythm

Chords

More

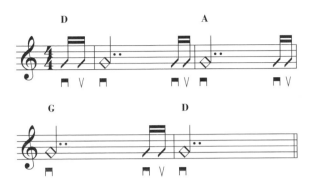

ABOVE: This typical rock strumming pattern is essentially just one strum per measure. What makes it distinctive is the rapid down-up 'pre-strum' before the main beat. These 'pre-strums' do not need to be played across all the strings, and open strings can be used on the second of them to help get to the main chord quickly.

Basics

Folk

Blues

Rock
'n'Roll

Pop
Rock

Heavy
Rock

Alt.
Rock

Other
Styles

Skills

Rhythm

Chords

More

Patterns in This Book

Opposite you will see some examples of the strumming patterns in this book. Many of the various features shown have been covered in this rhythm chapter.

The top example shows a basic strum pattern, with upstrums and downstrums marked by the arrows over the relevant strings. The numbers below refer to the counting rhythm.

The bottom example applies the pattern to a particular chord. You will see that the rhythm has been marked above the TAB, and particular notes indicated by the numbers on the TAB.

P.M. refers to 'palm mute'. The dot beside the second note means this note is half its length again: three semiquavers in this case. Double dots at the start and end are repeat signs.

Blues
Strum Pattern 3

Basics

Folk

Blues

Rock
'n'Roll

Pop
Rock

Heavy
Rock

Alt.
Rock

Other
Styles

Skills

Rhythm

Chords

More

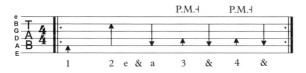

Pattern 3 on an E7 chord:

11

Chords

In the examples in this book you'll have
come across a number of different chords.
This chapter looks at what chords are and
provides a reference of useful chords and
keys. You'll also find more information on
chord charts, chord progressions, and chord
embellishments, to help add variety to your
rhythm playing.

Basics

Folk

Blues

Rock
'n'Roll

Pop
Rock

Heavy
Rock

Alt.
Rock

Other
Styles

Skills

Rhythm

Chords

More

Basics

Folk

Blues

Rock
'n'Roll

Pop
Rock

Heavy
Rock

Alt.
Rock

Other
Styles

Skills

Rhythm

Chords

More

Chords, Keys and Scales

Generally speaking, music in a certain key mostly uses chords that are made up using the notes of the scale of that key.

The **key** of a song refers to its overall tonality, and tells you which scale will be used as the basis of its melody and which chords fit naturally within it.

A **scale** is a set of ordered pitches in a key. Different scales produce different tonalities, but they follow patterns that can be applied to each key.

A **chord** simply refers to different notes sounded together. In their most basic form, chords are formed of three notes, called a **triad**.

To find the root position triads in each key, you go two steps up the scale to find the second note and then two more steps to find the third.

Basics

Folk

Blues

Rock 'n'Roll

Pop Rock

Heavy Rock

Alt. Rock

Other Styles

Skills

Rhythm

Chords

More

Common D major chords are derived
from the scale of D major

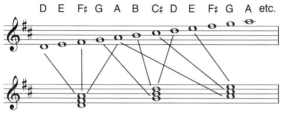

D major chord   G major chord   A major chord

Chords in a certain key can be worked out from the scale by
selecting a note and finding the note two steps higher in the
scale and the note two steps higher than that.

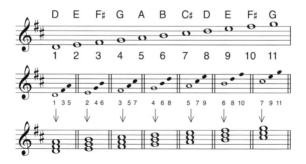

Basics

Folk

Blues

Rock
'n'Roll

Pop
Rock

Heavy
Rock

Alt.
Rock

Other
Styles

Skills

Rhythm

Chords

More

Chord Symbols

There are two main types of chords that form the core of most popular music: major chords and minor chords. Major chords have a bright, strong sound and minor chords have a mellow, sombre sound.

The chord symbol for major chords is simply the letter name of the chord written as a capital. For example, the chord symbol for the G major chord is 'G'.

Minor chord symbols consist of the capital letter of the chord name followed by a lowercase 'm'. For example, the chord symbol for the E minor chord is 'Em'.

Other chord types tend to just extend or vary the notes of the major or minor triads using other notes from the key. Opposite is a list of common chord types and their symbols shown for the key of C.

Chord Name	Chord Symbol	Chord Notes
C major	**C**	C, E, G
C minor	**Cm**	C, E♭, G
C augmented triad	**C+**	C, E, G♯
C diminished triad	**C°**	C, E♭, G♭
C suspended 2nd	**Csus2**	C, D, G
C suspended 4th	**Csus4**	C, F, G
C 5th (power) chord	**C5**	C, G
C major 6th	**C6**	C, E, G, A
C minor 6th	**Cm6**	C, E♭, G, A
C dominant 7th	**C7**	C, E, G, B♭
C major 7th	**Cmaj7**	C, E, G, B
C minor 7th	**Cm7**	C, E♭, G, B♭
C half diminished 7th	**C⌀7 or Cm7♭5**	C, E♭, G♭, B♭
C diminished 7th	**C°7**	C, E♭, G♭, B♭♭
C minor major 7th	**Cm(maj7)**	C, E♭, G, B
C dominant 7th ♯5	**C7+5**	C, E, G♯, B♭
C dominant 7th ♭5	**C7♭5**	C, E, G♭, B♭
C major add 9	**Cadd9**	C, E, G, D
C dominant 9th	**C9**	C, E, G, B♭, D
C major 9th	**Cmaj9**	C, E, G, B, D
C minor 9th	**Cm9**	C, E♭, G, B♭, D
C dominant 11th	**C11**	C, E, G, B♭, D, F
C dominant 13th	**C13**	C, E, G, B♭, D, A

Basics

Folk

Blues

Rock 'n'Roll

Pop Rock

Heavy Rock

Alt. Rock

Other Styles

Skills

Rhythm

Chords

More

Basics

Folk

Blues

Rock
'n'Roll

Pop
Rock

Heavy
Rock

Alt.
Rock

Other
Styles

Skills

Rhythm

Chords

More

Chord Symbol Variations

You may come across chord symbol notation where a chord name, such as G (G major), or C (C major) is written above the song lyrics in a different way. For example, C/E (C major with E as the lowest note) or C/G (C major with G as the lowest note) – these are inversions.

Every chord has a unique sound. This comes not only from the notes within the chord, such as C, E and G in a C major chord, but also from the order that the notes appear from bottom to top (for instance E C G), from the register they are in (high, middle or low), the way they are spaced (wide apart or close together) and repeated (for instance having two C's in the chord rather than one).

Sometimes chord symbols can't be detailed enough for this, so it's helpful to look at the spread of the notes in the stave or TAB notation too.

Chords

A C major chord consists of the notes C, E and G

These three notes can appear in a different order from bottom to top

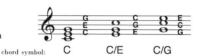

chord symbol: C   C/E   C/G

The chord can be written in different registers

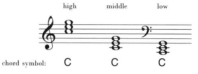

chord symbol: C   C   C

The chord can be spaced in different ways

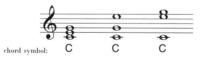

chord symbol: C   C   C

The chord can use the same note more than once

chord symbol: C   C   C

Basics

Folk

Blues

Rock 'n'Roll

Pop Rock

Heavy Rock

Alt. Rock

Other Styles

Skills

Rhythm

Chords

More

Basics

Folk

Blues

Rock
'n'Roll

Pop
Rock

Heavy
Rock

Alt.
Rock

Other
Styles

Skills

Rhythm

Chords

More

Key Signatures

The key of a piece of music determines the main
notes that will be included in it. In music notation
a key signature is written at the beginning of every
line of music to indicate the key.

Key signatures make music easier to read because
any sharps or flats in the key need only be written
at the start of each line and will then apply to
all those notes throughout the piece, rather than
needing to write a sharp or flat sign every time
such a note occurs.

Each major key has a unique key signature,
consisting of a collection of sharps or flats written
in a set order; these sharps and flats match those
that occur in the major scale for that key.

The key of C major contains no sharps or flats, so
the key signature is blank.

336

Basics

Folk

Blues

Rock
'n'Roll

Pop
Rock

Heavy
Rock

Alt.
Rock

Other
Styles

Skills

Rhythm

Chords

More

Key signatures are written at the beginning of a stave after
the clef and before the time signature

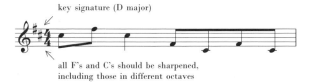

key signature (D major)

all F's and C's should be sharpened,
including those in different octaves

the actual notes to be played:

Natural signs need to be used if an unaltered version of a note
in the key signature is to be played

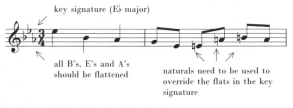

key signature (E♭ major)

all B's, E's and A's
should be flattened

naturals need to be used to
override the flats in the key
signature

the actual notes to be played:

Basics

Folk

Blues

Rock 'n'Roll

Pop Rock

Heavy Rock

Alt. Rock

Other Styles

Skills

Rhythm

Chords

More

Basics

Folk

Blues

Rock
'n'Roll

Pop
Rock

Heavy
Rock

Alt.
Rock

Other
Styles

Skills

Rhythm

Chords

More

Keys

The 'key' of a song refers to its overall tonality, and dictates which scale will be used as the basis of the melody and which chords fit naturally into the arrangement. Understanding which chords go together in a key will help you work out the chord structure of songs, and will provide a framework to begin writing your own songs.

Major Keys

In each major key, three major chords occur – as shown below:

Key	Major Chords in the Key
C major	C F G
G major	G C D
D major	D G A
A major	A D E

Basics

Folk

Blues

Rock
'n'Roll

Pop
Rock

Heavy
Rock

Alt.
Rock

Other
Styles

Skills

Rhythm

Chords

More

A song or chord progression will normally begin with the tonic (keynote) chord. This is the chord that has the same name as the key. For example, in the key of C major, C is the tonic (keynote) chord.

Minor chords also occur in major keys. Some of the most commonly used minor chords in the keys of C, D, E, F and G major are shown below.

Key	Minor Chords in the Key		
C major	Dm	Em	Am
G major	Am	Bm	Em
D major	Em	F♯m	Bm
A major	Bm	Dm	F♯m
E major	F♯m	G♯m	C♯m

Although there are no fixed rules about which chords can be combined when you are composing a song or chord progression, if you select chords from the same key they will always fit together well. On the opposite page is an example of a chord progression using chords in the key of C major.

Basics

Folk

Blues

Rock
'n'Roll

Pop
Rock

Heavy
Rock

Alt.
Rock

Other
Styles

Skills

Rhythm

Chords

More

|| C | Dm | Em | F |

| Am | G | F | C ||

ABOVE: Chord progression in the key of C major.

Minor Keys

In each minor key, three minor chords are closely related, and most commonly occur in popular songs. For example, in the key of A minor the chords of Am, Dm and Em are the most important. Three major chords also occur in each minor key. For example, in the key of A minor, C, F and G major chords occur. As all these chords are within the same key they can be combined in any order (after starting with the tonic/keynote chord) to make a pleasant-sounding chord sequence.

An example is shown on the following page, but you can experiment with rearranging the chords in

Basics

Folk

Blues

Rock 'n'Roll

Pop Rock

Heavy Rock

Alt. Rock

Other Styles

Skills

Rhythm

Chords

More

a different order and then playing them through to hear the musical result.

Here are a few chord progressions demonstrating some of the most common chord sequences used in a few of the most popular major and minor keys.

‖ Am | F | G | C |

| Am | Dm | Em | Am ‖

ABOVE: Chord progression in the key of A minor.

‖ G | D | C | G |

| Em | Am | D | G ‖

ABOVE: Chord progression in the key of G major.

‖ D | Em | F♯m | Em |

| G | A | G | D ‖

ABOVE: Chord progression in the key of D major.

Basics

Folk

Blues

Rock 'n'Roll

Pop Rock

Heavy Rock

Alt. Rock

Other Styles

Skills

Rhythm

Chords

More

```
|| C  | G  | Am | Am |
|  F  | Em | Dm | C  ||
```

ABOVE: Chord progression in the key of C major.

```
|| A  | E  | F#m | E  |
|  D  | E  | A   | A  ||
```

ABOVE: Chord progression in the key of A major.

```
|| Em | D  | C  | D  |
|  Am | G  | D  | Em ||
```

ABOVE: Chord progression in the key of E minor.

Am

G

D

Em

Useful Chord Diagrams

Some keys and chords are more common than others. You're most likely to use and come across the following popular major keys:

- **C major**
- **D major**
- **E major**
- **G major**
- **A major**

Chord diagrams for the major root position triads for these five keys are shown on the following pages for reference. The QR codes link to our website flametreemusic.com, where you can hear how each chord sounds on the guitar, both as a strummed chord and an arpeggio.

C
Major

Basics

Folk

Blues

Rock 'n'Roll

Pop Rock

Heavy Rock

Alt. Rock

Other Styles

Skills

Rhythm

Chords

More

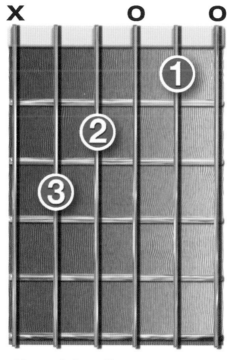

X   O   O

Chord Spelling

1st (C), 3rd (E), 5th (G)

D
Major

X   X   O

Chord Spelling

1st (D), 3rd (F♯), 5th (A)

E
Major

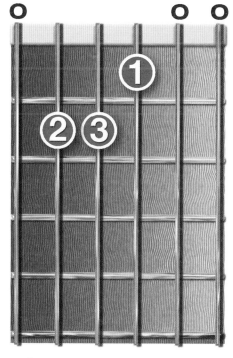

Basics

Folk

Blues

Rock 'n'Roll

Pop Rock

Heavy Rock

Alt. Rock

Other Styles

Skills

Rhythm

Chords

More

Chord Spelling

1st (E), 3rd (G♯), 5th (B)

Basics

Folk

Blues

Rock 'n'Roll

Pop Rock

Heavy Rock

Alt. Rock

Other Styles

Skills

Rhythm

Chords

More

G
Major

Chord Spelling

1st (G), 3rd (B), 5th (D)

A
Major

X   O   O

① ② ③

Chord Spelling

1st (A), 3rd (C♯), 5th (E)

Basics

Folk

Blues

Rock 'n' Roll

Pop Rock

Heavy Rock

Alt. Rock

Other Styles

Skills

Rhythm

Chords

More

Basics

Folk

Blues

Rock 'n'Roll

Pop Rock

Heavy Rock

Alt. Rock

Other Styles

Skills

Rhythm

Chords

More

Sevenths

Seventh chords are the most common extension to basic triad chords. They are very common in music and there are three different types:

- Major Sevenths
- Dominant Sevenths
- Minor Sevenths

Major seventh chords consist of a major seventh interval. This is the interval from the first to the seventh note of the major scale.

If you lower the major seventh interval by a half step it becomes a minor seventh. This interval occurs in both minor 7th and dominant 7th chords. The quality of the 3rd determines whether the chord is a minor 7th or dominant 7th: dominant 7th chords include a major third, but in minor 7th chords the 3rd is minor too.

350

Major 7th	Chord Notes
Cmaj7	C, E, G, B
Dmaj7	D, F♯, A, C♯
Emaj7	E, G♯, B, D♯
Fmaj7	F, A, C, E
Gmaj7	G, B, D, F♯
Amaj7	A, C♯, E, G♯
Bmaj7	B, D♯, F♯, A♯

Basics
Folk
Blues
Rock 'n'Roll
Pop Rock
Heavy Rock
Alt. Rock
Other Styles
Skills
Rhythm
Chords
More

Cmaj7
Major 7th

1st (C), 3rd (E), 5th (G), 7th (B)

Gmaj7
Major 7th

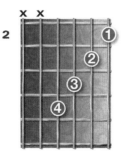

1st (G), 3rd (B), 5th (D), 7th (F♯)

Basics

Folk

Blues

Rock
'n'Roll

Pop
Rock

Heavy
Rock

Alt.
Rock

Other
Styles

Skills

Rhythm

Chords

More

Dominant 7th	Chord Notes
C7	C, E, G, B♭
D7	D, F♯, A, C
E7	E, G♯, B, D
F7	F, A, C, E♭
G7	G, B, D, F
A7	A, C♯, E, G
B7	B, D♯, F♯, A

C7
Dominant 7th

1st (C), 3rd (E), 5th (G), ♭7th (B♭)

G7
Dominant 7th

1st (G), 3rd (B), 5th (D), ♭7th (F)

Minor 7th	Chord Notes
Cm7	C, E♭, G, B♭
Dm7	D, F, A, C
Em7	E, G, B, D
Fm7	F, A♭, C, E♭
Gm7	G, B♭, D, F
Am7	A, C, E, G
Bm7	B, D, F♯, A

Cm7
Minor 7th

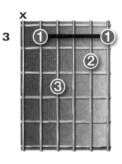

Gm7
Minor 7th

1st (C), ♭3rd (E♭), 5th (G), ♭7th (B♭)   1st (G), ♭3rd (B♭), 5th (D), ♭7th (F)

Basics

Folk

Blues

Rock
'n'Roll

Pop
Rock

Heavy
Rock

Alt.
Rock

Other
Styles

Skills

Rhythm

Chords

More

Chord Charts

Simple chord charts are the most commonly used way of notating the chord structure of a song or progression.

If you audition for a pop or rock band, the music you'll be asked to play will most likely be presented as a simple chord chart.

Reading Chord Charts

A chord chart normally has the time signature written at the very beginning. If there is no time signature then it's usually safe to assume that the music is in $\frac{4}{4}$ time.

Each measure is separated by a vertical line, with two vertical lines indicating the end of the piece. Chord symbols are used to show which chords should be played.

Split Measures

When more than one chord appears in a single
measure it can be assumed that the measure is to
be evenly divided between the chords that appear
within it. In a song in $\frac{3}{4}$ time, if three chords all
appear in the same measure then you can assume
that the measure is to be divided equally – with one
beat per chord.

$$\| \frac{4}{4} \quad C \quad | \quad Am \quad | \quad Dm \quad | \quad G \quad |$$
$$| \quad F \quad | \quad Em \quad | \quad G \quad | \quad C \quad \|$$

$$\| \frac{3}{4} \quad C \quad | \quad Am \quad |$$
$$| \quad Em \quad F \quad G \quad | \quad C \quad \|$$

ABOVE: In the penultimate measure, each chord lasts
for one beat.

Basics

Folk

Blues

Rock
'n'Roll

Pop
Rock

Heavy
Rock

Alt.
Rock

Other
Styles

Skills

Rhythm

Chords

More

 In many chord charts, in order to make the
intention clear and avoid confusion, any division
within a measure is shown by either a dot or a
diagonal line after each chord: each dot or diagonal
line indicates another beat.

$$\| \; ^4_4 \; C \; / \; Am \; / \; | Dm \; / \; G \; / \; |$$
$$| \; F \; / \; Em \; / \; | \; G \; / \; C \; / \; \|$$

ABOVE: Each chord lasts for two beats: one beat indicated
by the chord symbol and an additional beat indicated by
the diagonal line.

$$\| \; ^4_4 \; C \; Em \; / \; / \; | \; F \; G \; / \; / \; |$$
$$| \; Am \; Em \; / \; / \; | \; G \; C \; / \; / \; \|$$

ABOVE: In this example, the first chord in each measure lasts for
just one beat and the second chord lasts for three beats.

Basics

Folk

Blues

Rock
'n'Roll

Pop
Rock

Heavy
Rock

Alt.
Rock

Other
Styles

Skills

Rhythm

Chords

More

‖ $\frac{4}{4}$ C . . Dm | Em . . F |

| Dm . . G | F . . C ‖

ABOVE: Here, instead of diagonal lines, dots are used to show the rhythmic divisions within each measure. The first chord in each measure lasts for three beats and the second chord lasts for one beat.

Interpreting Chord Charts

In standard chord charts, while the duration of each chord is clearly shown, the rhythm style that should be played is left to the discretion of the performer.

In theory this means that you could interpret the chart in any way you wish in terms of the number of strums per beat, however you should make sure that your rhythm playing relates to the musical style and mood of the song.

Basics

Folk

Blues

Rock
'n'Roll

Pop
Rock

Heavy
Rock

Alt.
Rock

Other
Styles

Skills

Rhythm

Chords

More

Following Chord Charts

If every bar of a whole song were written out in a chord chart it would take up several pages and become cumbersome to read. Instead chord charts are normally abbreviated by using a number of 'repeat symbols'. In order to follow a chord chart accurately it is essential to understand what each repeat symbol means.

Repeat Symbols

✕. This symbol is used when one bar is to be repeated exactly.

²✕. This symbol is used when more than one bar is to be repeated.

The number of bars to be repeated is written above the symbol.

BELOW: Here is an example of these symbols in use.

should be played as

Basics

Folk

Blues

Rock 'n'Roll

Pop Rock

Heavy Rock

Alt. Rock

Other Styles

Skills

Rhythm

Chords

More

Basics

Folk

Blues

Rock
'n'Roll

Pop
Rock

Heavy
Rock

Alt.
Rock

Other
Styles

Skills

Rhythm

Chords

More

Section Repeats

The symbol of a double barline followed by two dots indicates the start of a section, and the symbol of two dots followed by a double barline indicates the end of the section to be repeated. If there are no dots at the start of the section, then repeat the music from the beginning of the piece. If the section is to be repeated more than once, the number of times it is to be played is written above the last repeat symbol.

If two sections of music are identical, except for the last measure or measures, repeat dots are used in conjunction with first-time and second-time ending directions, as shown opposite.

should be played as

$$\|\; {\textstyle\frac{4}{4}}\; Am \;|\; G \;|\; F \;|\; Em \;|\; Am \;|$$
$$|\; G \;|\; F \;|\; Dm \;|\; Am \;\|$$

As well as repeat dots there are several other commonly used repeat signs:

- **D.C.** (an abbreviation of *Da Capo*) means play 'from the beginning'. For example, if the entire piece of music is to be repeated, D.C. can be written at the end to instruct you to play it again from the beginning.

- **D.S.** (an abbreviation of *Dal Segno*) means play 'from the sign': 𝄋 . For example, if the verse and chorus of a song are to be repeated, but not the

Basics

Folk

Blues

Rock
'n'Roll

Pop
Rock

Heavy
Rock

Alt.
Rock

Other
Styles

Skills

Rhythm

Chords

More

Basics

Folk

Blues

Rock 'n'Roll

Pop Rock

Heavy Rock

Alt. Rock

Other Styles

Skills

Rhythm

Chords

More

introduction, **D.S.** can be written at the end of the music with the D.S. sign written at the start of the verse. This instructs the performer to start again from the sign.

- **Coda** is the musical term for the end section of a piece of music. The start of the coda is marked by the sign: $\oplus$.

- **Fine** is the musical term for the end of a piece of music.

Some of the above repeat signs might be combined in a chord chart.

Fine

‖ $\frac{4}{4}$ Em | Am | D | Em ‖

D.C. al Fine

| G | C | D | D ‖

ABOVE: In this example, after eight measures repeat from the beginning and then end after measure four where the sign 'Fine' appears.

Basics

Folk

Blues

Rock
'n'Roll

Pop
Rock

Heavy
Rock

Alt.
Rock

Other
Styles

Skills

Rhythm

Chords

More

ABOVE: In this example, after eight measures repeat from the beginning and then after measure four jump to the coda section.

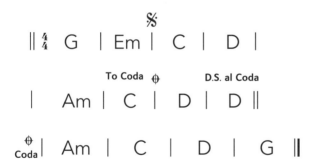

ABOVE: In this example, after eight measures repeat from the start of measure three to the end of measure six, then jump to the coda section.

Chord Progressions

I vi IV V

This incredibly popular chord progression can be found in many of the songs around today. It uses four chords, based on roman numerals applied to the key's scale. Upper-case numerals refer to major chords, and lower-case numerals refer to minor chords. In C, the I vi IV V refers to C, G, Am and F.

I V vi IV

A different ordering of the same chords was immensely popular in the 20th century, and is now often referred to as the "50s" chord progression. The most popular form of the I vi IV V progression uses a V7 chord. This is a simple but effective variation of the basic progression. A V7 refers to a dominant 7th chord: the initial V triad is major, and the 7th note is minor. In C major, this would be G7.

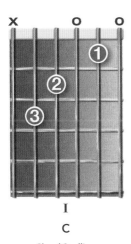

I

C

Chord Spelling
1st (C), 3rd (E), 5th (G)

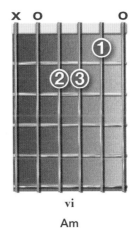

vi

Am

Chord Spelling
1st (A), ♭3rd (C), 5th (E)

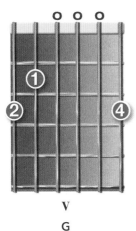

V

G

Chord Spelling
1st (G), 3rd (B), 5th (D)

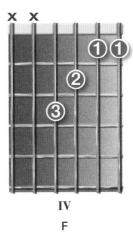

IV

F

Chord Spelling
1st (F), 3rd (A), 5th (C)

Basics

Folk

Blues

Rock
'n'Roll

Pop
Rock

Heavy
Rock

Alt.
Rock

Other
Styles

Skills

Rhythm

Chords

More

Basics

Folk

Blues

Rock
'n'Roll

Pop
Rock

Heavy
Rock

Alt.
Rock

Other
Styles

Skills

Rhythm

Chords

More

The I IV V Progression

Another very common chord progression is the
I IV V. It uses the 'primary chords' of a key, which
are frequently used because of their strong harmonic
links with one another.

In blues music, the same chord progression is used to
great effect with dominant 7th chords instead of the
basic triads.

In the key of C Major, I IV V refers to the chords
C, F and G.

Presented as a simple chord chart, and assuming
standard 4/4 timing with four beats per bar:

| C / / / |
| F / / / |
| G / / / |

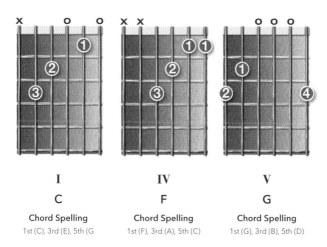

I	IV	V
C	F	G
Chord Spelling	**Chord Spelling**	**Chord Spelling**
1st (C), 3rd (E), 5th (G	1st (F), 3rd (A), 5th (C)	1st (G), 3rd (B), 5th (D)

The Twelve-bar Blues

Perhaps most famously, the I IV V progression forms the basis of the twelve-bar blues. This can take various forms, with a typical example being:

I	I	I	I
IV	IV	I	I
V	IV	I	I

It's common to use 7ths here too, so play around with I7, IV7 and V7 variants to get the effect you want.

Basics

Folk

Blues

Rock 'n'Roll

Pop Rock

Heavy Rock

Alt. Rock

Other Styles

Skills

Rhythm

Chords

More

Basics

Folk

Blues

Rock
'n'Roll

Pop
Rock

Heavy
Rock

Alt.
Rock

Other
Styles

Skills

Rhythm

Chords

More

Adding Structure:
Moving Bass Lines

A way to add structure to a chord progression is to add a moving bass line. To move neatly in small steps usually involves inverted (or slash) chords.

Ascending and Descending Basslines

Also known as a 'walking bass', a descending bassline moves down in steps. A simple example could involve an inverted G/B chord to give a B in the bass, placed between a root position C and an A chord. Ascending basslines go in the opposite direction, stepping up instead of down.

Alternating Bassline

An alternating bass involves a return to the same bass note, usually every other chord, to deliver a strong sense of rhythm. An example can be found opposite, where the bass moves back and forth between D and A, then B and F♯.

♩=140

let ring throughout

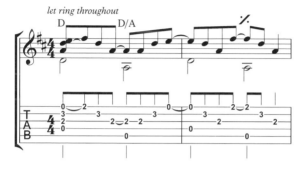

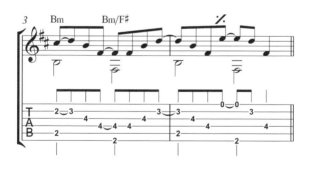

Basics

Folk

Blues

Rock
'n'Roll

Pop
Rock

Heavy
Rock

Alt.
Rock

Other
Styles

Skills

Rhythm

Chords

More

Adding Variety

There are many different ways of playing the same chord, so making chord strumming sound good is often a case of choosing the musical and rhythmic features that best suit your needs at the time. You might want to embellish an existing chord sequence, swap to a different chord, or play with the timing.

Developing Riffs

A riff is a short musical phrase that is repeated throughout a song, and is often what hooks a listener in. This is likely to include a chord progression movement of some kind, even if all the chord notes aren't played.

Extended/Altered Chords

Using extended or altered chords is a sure way to add variety to an otherwise basic chord sequence.

Basics

Folk

Blues

Rock 'n'Roll

Pop Rock

Heavy Rock

Alt. Rock

Other Styles

Skills

Rhythm

Chords

More

Passing Notes

You may want to use the scale you're in to include a few notes between chords. The chromatic scale (see page 374) is a useful scale to know if you'd like to include notes that aren't in the scale too.

Timing and Rhythm

Using chords of different lengths is one way to play with the timing of your progression. A combination of short and long notes, while still keeping a regular rhythm, helps create a distinctive stylistic rhythm.

Syncopation, which shifts the emphasis of beats in a measure away from the obvious timing, is another useful technique to try out.

Rests between chords help add a well-defined rhythm to your progression, giving it musical shape and character.

Basics

Folk

Blues

Rock
'n'Roll

Pop
Rock

Heavy
Rock

Alt.
Rock

Other
Styles

Skills

Rhythm

Chords

More

Octaves

If you play a scale from the lowest note on the
guitar to the highest, you will find that each
note reappears at regular intervals. This occurs
because the 7 whole note names from A to G
are repeated.

The interval, or distance, between two note pitches
of the same name is called an octave.

Knowledge of octaves is useful because it gives
you a wider sonic range to play across – from deep
bassy riffs to high-pitched screaming solos.

It also gives you more options when playing chords.
Choosing the same note at a different pitch or
octave allows you to get the particular sound you
want, and also might mean the chord is in an easier
position to play, making the process of strumming
it even simpler.

Chords

C D E F G A B C D E F G A B

These notes reappear further up the stave

Each of these pairs of notes contain an octave

C C D D E E F F G G A A B B

Basics

Folk

Blues

Rock
'n'Roll

Pop
Rock

Heavy
Rock

Alt.
Rock

Other
Styles

Skills

Rhythm

Chords

More

The Chromatic Scale

This scale contains every half step between the starting note and the octave. It can be used with any chord and covers every note on the fretboard.

It is the only 12-note scale in music and does not relate to any particular key. Instead, when improvising, notes from the chromatic scale can be added to introduce notes that are not in the key of the backing. These extra notes are called 'accidentals' and can help add colour to an arrangement.

As it contains all twelve semitones it is useful to be aware of this scale to give maximum flexibility to your chord and solo-playing. Including these 'outside' notes as chromatic passing notes within a lead-guitar solo or over the top of chords can help provide moments of harmonic tension.

Chords

Basics

Folk

Blues

Rock 'n'Roll

Pop Rock

Heavy Rock

Alt. Rock

Other Styles

Skills

Rhythm

Chords

More

Basics

Folk

Blues

Rock
'n'Roll

Pop
Rock

Heavy
Rock

Alt.
Rock

Other
Styles

Skills

Rhythm

Chords

More

Strumming Patterns
in Action

Opposite you will find a full notated example of
one of the strumming patterns in this book. They
are shown in both standard and TAB notation,
with chord boxes included on the musical examples
where possible. If these are not given there are
useful chords at the back of each example chapter.

This example is from the Pop Rock section of this
book, and shows a very popular chord progression
in C major. The X's refer to muted notes.

For more on keys, see pages 337–334.

For chord symbol notation, see pages 333–336.

For chord progressions, see pages 365–370.

For a reminder of note values, see pages 253–274
in the Rhythm chapter.

Pop-Rock
Example with
I V vi IV Progression

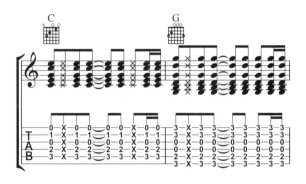

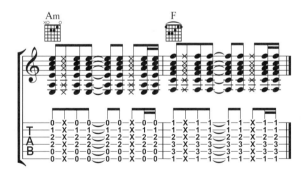

Basics

Folk

Blues

Rock 'n'Roll

Pop Rock

Heavy Rock

Alt. Rock

Other Styles

Skills

Rhythm

Chords

More

Basics

Folk

Blues

Rock
'n'Roll

Pop
Rock

Heavy
Rock

Alt.
Rock

Other
Styles

Skills

Rhythm

Chords

More

12

More Resources

Our website flametreemusic.com contains
diagrams and audio links for guitar chords and
scales. Included in this section is a glossary of
useful definitions for some of the terms used
in this book, and we also have a collection of
other music guides that could come in useful if
you intend to develop your skills playing and
songwriting for the guitar.

Basics

Folk

Blues

Rock
'n'Roll

Pop
Rock

Heavy
Rock

Alt.
Rock

Other
Styles

Skills

Rhythm

Chords

More

Glossary

Arpeggio The sounding of the notes of a chord in succession rather than all simultaneously. These can be played individually while holding a chord down or by picking out the notes separately on the fingerboard.

Barre Chord A chord where one of a guitarist's fretting fingers (usually the first finger) is held down across many or all of the strings in addition to other fingers holding down separate notes.

Bottleneck A technique in which a player moves a glass or metal bar up and down the guitar neck while playing, to produce sliding pitches.

Double-stop A two-note chord, melody or phrase.

Finger-style While most rock and pop guitarists play their instruments with a plectrum, all classical and flamenco guitar players articulate their notes with the separate fingers and thumb of their right hand (or left hand if playing left-handed). These players use their thumb to play the bass notes, usually with downstrokes on the bottom three strings, and their first, second and third fingers to play the other strings.

Flatpicking A style where all notes, scalar and chordal, are articulated with a plectrum.

Glissando When a guitarist plays a glissando, they are sliding up or down the guitar neck in such a way that every note under the left-hand finger is articulated. This is different from a basic slide, in which the only notes that can be clearly heard are the first and last notes played by the left-hand finger.

Hammer-on A technique in which you play a note behind a fret on the fingerboard and then hammer one of your other fingers down behind another fret higher up on the same string.

Palm Muting You can mute a guitar's strings by placing your right hand lightly across them. This is very useful if you're playing at high volume and don't want the strings to ring out unnecessarily. It can also be used to add more colour and texture to a rhythm or solo.

Pull-off A pull-off can be seen as the reverse of a hammer-on. In this case, a note is played and then the finger playing that note is pulled off the string to sound a lower note that is either an open string or one fretted by another finger.

Riff A riff is a short series of chords or notes that can be repeated to form a catchy sequence.

Semitone The smallest interval between two notes on a fretted guitar. Notes on either side of a fret are separated by a semitone (S). An interval of two semitones is called a tone (T).

Slide An effect produced when you play one note on the guitar and, while still holding the note down, slide up or down the guitar neck to another note. In a true slide, the only two notes you can hear clearly are the first and last notes, at the beginning and end of the slide, whereas a glissando is a sliding effect played so that every note under the finger is articulated.

Time Signature A time signature is a sign placed after the clef at the beginning of a piece of music to indicate its meter.

Triad Basic three-note chords that are also the building blocks of most other chords.

Basics
Folk
Blues
Rock 'n'Roll
Pop Rock
Heavy Rock
Alt. Rock
Other Styles
Skills
Rhythm
Chords
More

Other Guides

Here are a few companion titles that could come in useful if you intend to develop your skills playing and songwriting for the guitar or piano.

Guitar Chords

Our bestselling chord book is a comprehensive reference tool for guitarists of any ability. Contains 360 chords, one chord per page, divided by key.

Popular Chords

Popular chords and how to use them: covering the most common chord progressions and examples of them in use, with audio at flametreemusic.com.

Basics

Folk

Blues

Rock 'n'Roll

Pop Rock

Heavy Rock

Alt. Rock

Other Styles

Skills

Rhythm

Chords

More

Scales for Great Solos

A guide to the most common scales in all keys, with links to flametreemusic.com throughout. Includes tips on soloing and the best scales to use for different chords and music styles.

Guitar Chords Card Pack

A pack of cards introducing common chord structures and encouraging

experimentation with popular chords. One clear guitar

diagram per card and small instruction booklet included.

FLAME TREE | PUBLISHING
MUSIC PORTAL

Hear Chords and Scales
FLAMETREEMUSIC.COM

Expert Music Information
FLAMETREEPRO.COM

Sheet Music Playlists
FLAMETREEPIANO.COM

The **FLAME TREE MUSIC PORTAL** brings **chords**
and **scales** you can see *and* hear, an **Expert Music
search engine** on a wide range of genres, styles,
artists and instruments, and free access to **playlists**
for our sheet music series.

Other FLAME TREE music books include:

The Jazz and Blues Encyclopedia (Editor: Howard Mandel)
Definitive Opera Encyclopedia (Founding Editor: Stanley Sadie)
Advanced Guitar Chords by Jake Jackson
Beginners Guide to Reading Music by Jake Jackson
Sheet Music for Piano: Scott Joplin by Alan Brown

See our full range of books at **flametreepublishing.com**